CATALOGUE
OF ANCIENT SCULPTURES
I
Aegean, Cypriote, and Graeco-Phoenician

THE NATIONAL MUSEUM OF DENMARK
Department of Near Eastern and Classical Antiquities

CATALOGUE
OF ANCIENT SCULPTURES
I

Aegean, Cypriote, and Graeco-Phoenician
by
P.J. Riis, Mette Moltesen, and Pia Guldager

Copenhagen 1989

© The National Museum of Denmark.
Department of Near Eastern and Classical Antiquities.

The English was revised by Mr. Geoffrey Bibby.

The publication was sponsored by The Ny Carlsberg Foundation
and Consul General Gösta Enboms Foundation.

Publications of The Department of Near Eastern and Classical
Antiquities, The National Museum of Denmark.

Photographer: Lennart Larsen
Designer: Jørgen Levinsen
General Editor: Søren Dietz

ISBN 87-89438-01-9

Printed in Denmark by Special-Trykkeriet Viborg a-s

CONTENTS

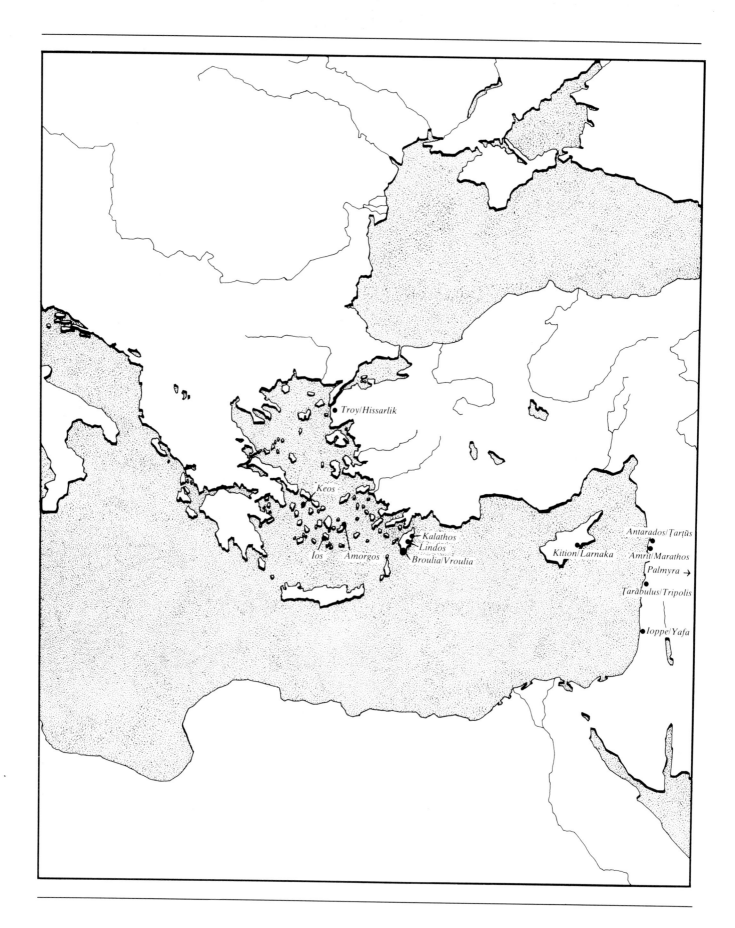

Troy/Hissarlik

Keos

Kalathos
Lindos
Ios   Amorgos
Broulia/Vroulia

Antarados/Tarṭūs
Kition/Larnaka   Amrit/Marathos
Palmyra →
Tarābulus/Tripolis

Ioppe/Yafa

PREFACE

For quite a long time Classical archaeologists, particulary those working in other countries, have felt the lack of a scholarly catalogue of the ancient sculptures in the National Museum of Denmark. Although not to be compared with the rich collection in the Ny Carlsberg Glyptotek, the National Museum's sculptures, of which the greater part comes from the old Royal Art Cabinet and other Royal collections, have a special value, inasmuch as they form a small chapter of Denmark's own cultural history through 300 years, showing how, in this country, an interest in ancient plastic arts was created and developed, and showing who was instrumental in bringing this about and making such art known to the Danish public.

Therefore, in the 1940s, on the advice of the Director General of Antiquities and Cultural Museums, Dr. Poul Nørlund, of the Professor of Classical Archaeology in the University of Copenhagen, Dr. K. Friis Johansen, and of the Director of the Ny Carlsberg Glyptotek, Dr. Vagn Poulsen, the present writer, then Keeper of the National Museum's Department of Near Eastern and Classical Antiquities, began working on a catalogue raisonné based on the same principles as the series "Publications de la Glyptothèque Ny-Carlsberg" which was planned about the same time, and whose first volume appeared in 1948. However, the professorship to which I was appointed in 1949 left me little time for continuing this work, and even after having succeeded Professor Friis Johansen in 1956 my different tasks made it difficult to complete even one minor part of the catalogue. In 1977 the situation improved, and, thanks to the cooperation of Mrs. Mette Moltesen, M.A., Keeper of Classical Art in the Ny Carlsberg Glyptotek, and to a personal grant from the Carlsberg Foundation securing for myself the help of Miss Pia Guldager, B.A., it has now been possible to complete this volume.

In 1949 I had finished a draft in Danish dealing with the Aegean, Cypriote, and Greek archaic and classical sculptures up to c. 400 B.C., a total of 101 items. In 1978 Mrs. Moltesen was given a copy of this draft, and it was agreed that she should help to revise the text and herself write the remaining part on the classical sculptures of the 4th century B.C. With due regard to her critical remarks I began in 1982 to bring the manuscript up to date and to translate it into English, but I have only made ready the Aegean, Cypriote and Graeco-Phoenician sections for publishing, as Mrs. Moltesen consented to take over the entire Greek archaic and classical material. Miss Guldager has assisted in checking the descriptions and references, and she has also made many corrections and additional remarks, particularly concerning the Aegean objects. We have made the bibliographies of the individual items nearly complete in order to demonstrate both the scholarly significance of the objects and the degree of artistic and public interest taken in them.

I am most grateful to my two collaborators, who have relieved me of a rather heavy task, and all three of us moreover wish to tender our sincere thanks to the staff of the Department of Near Eastern and Classical Antiquities, and to the photographers of the National Museum, for their valuable support. We also express our gratitude for generous help given by Dr. Poul Graff-Petersen of the Copenhagen University Museum of Geology, Professor Benedikt Otzen of Aarhus University, and the late sculptor Vitus Nielsen.

December, 1986   P.J.Riis

ABBREVIATIONS

In addition to those enumerated in the *Bibliographie des Jahrbuchs des deutschen archäologischen Instituts* the following abbreviations are used:

Aarb – Aarbøger for nordisk Oldkyndighed og Historie 1 ff, Copenhagen 1886 ff.

BMCoins – Catalogue of Greek Coins in the British Museum, London 1873 ff.

BMJewellery – Catalogue of the Jewellery, Greek, Etruscan, and Roman, in the Departments of Antiquities, British Museum, London 1911.

BMSculpture – Catalogue of Sculpture in the Department of Greek and Roman Antiquities of the British Museum I ff, London 1928 ff.

Buschor, AS – E. Buschor, Altsamische Standbilder I-V, Berlin 1934-61.

ClRh – Clara Rhodos 1-10, Bergamo 1928-41.

Cycladiaca – J.L. Fitton (ed.), Cycladiaca, London 1984.

Dörpfeld, T&I – W. Dörpfeld, Troja und Ilion I-II, Athens 1902.

FdB – M. Dunand et al., Fouilles de Byblos 1 ff, Paris 1939 ff.

Lindos – Lindos I-IV 1, Berlin & Copenhagen 1931 ff.

MémSocAntN – Mémoires de la Société royale des Antiquaires du Nord, Copenhagen 1836 ff.

ML – W.H. Roscher, Ausführliches Lexikon der griechischen und römischen Mythologie I-VI, Leipzig 1884-1937.

NMArb – Fra Nationalmuseets Arbejdsmark, Copenhagen 1928 ff.

NMFührer – Nationalmuseum, Führer durch die Antikensammlung[3], Copenhagen 1908.

NMSkr – Nationalmuseets Skrifter, arkæologisk-historisk række 1 ff. Copenhagen 1943 ff.

NMV – Nationalmuseets Vejledninger, Copenhagen.

NCGColl – From the Collections of the Ny Carlsberg Glyptothek 1 ff, Copenhagen 1931 ff.

Perrot & Chipiez – G. Perrot & C. Chipiez, Histoire de l'Art dans l'Antiquité I-X, Paris 1882-1914.

Phylakopi – Excavations at Phylakopi in Melos, JHSSupplPap 4, London 1904.

RDAC – Reports of the Department of Antiquities in Cyprus, Nicosia 1963 ff.

Richter, Korai – G.M.A. Richter, Korai, Archaic Greek Maidens, London 1968.

Richter, Kouroi – G.M.A. Richter, Kouroi, Archaic Greek Youths[3], London & New York 1970.

SCE – Swedish Cyprus Expedition I ff, Stockholm 1934 ff.

Schmidt, SS – H. Schmidt, Heinrich Schliemanns Sammlung trojanischer Altertümer, Berlin 1902.

SIMA – Studies in Mediterranean Archaeology I ff, Lund 1962 ff.

SNG – Sylloge Nummorum Graecorum, Danish National Museum 1-43, Copenhagen 1942-79.

Thimme – J. Thimme (ed.), Kunst und Kultur der Kykladen im Jahr 3000 vor Christus, Karlsruhe 1976.

Troy – Troy, Excavations Conducted by the University of Cincinnati I-IV, Princeton 1950-58.

Vroulia – K.F. Kinch, Fouilles de Vroulia, Berlin 1914.

Wiesner, GuJ – J. Wiesner, Grab und Jenseits, Religionsgeschichtliche Versuche und Vorarbeiten 26, Giessen 1938.

Xanthoudides – S. Xanthoudides, The Vaulted Tombs of Mesara, Liverpool & London 1924.

A SHORT HISTORY OF
THE COLLECTION OF SCULPTURES

The collections of the National Museum have their origin in the Royal Art Cabinet founded by King Frederik III in 1653. When it was dissolved in the early 19th century, the Near Eastern and Classical antiquities were in 1826 segregated as a separate department of the new Royal Museum of Art, and in 1851 they were united with the late king Christian VIII's private collection, thus forming an independent Royal Cabinet of Antiquities, later called the Royal Collection of Antiquities. In 1892 this was incorporated in the National Museum.

The earliest acquisitions of ancient sculpture must be viewed in a religious perspective. Just as the Protestant Danish nobles, who in the 16th and 17th centuries travelled to the Eastern Mediterranean, were mainly guided by a pious wish to visit the Holy Land, so the two Parthenon marbles (ABb 13 and 14a), which Captain Moritz Hartmann, a Danish officer serving in the Venetian navy, had bought in Athens, were in 1688 sent as a gift to his sovereign, the Danish King Christian V, in the belief that they came from the Artemis temple in Ephesos, well-known to good Christians from the 19th chapter in the Acts of the Apostles.

The autocratic rulers of the period, however, having Louis XIV of France as their model, not only attached importance to such objects with more or less sacred provenience; they also liked to possess portraits of the Roman emperors and their relatives. The most noble-minded of these were the radiant ideals of the kings and their family, whereas the history of the others without doubt could serve as a warning. It is symptomatic that one of the sculptures bought in the years between 1690 and 1737 was a bust held to represent Caesar, afterwards named Caligula, but really a posthumous portrait of Augustus (ABb 14b). Another was a head of the emperor Commodus as a young prince (ABb 5), and already before 1673, perhaps even in the days of Frederik III, the collection included a small female bust dating from the reign of Antoninus Pius, presumably regarded as the portrait of an empress or an imperial princess (ABb 8).

Three royal initiatives, although intended to glorify the monarch, indirectly changed the situation. They were Christian VI's creation of an Academy of Arts in 1738 and of an Academy of Sciences and Letters in 1742, and the establishment of a Foundation *ad usus publicos* by Frederik V in 1765, enlarged by his son Christian VII in 1779. Through these institutions artists and scholars obtained increasing influence upon the cultural development of the country, an influence which even extended to the care of the Royal Art Cabinet. After the middle of the century the governing principles little by little became purely artistic and antiquarian. This is borne out very clearly in the instructions which the Secretary of State, Ove Høegh Guldberg, himself an active collector, gave in 1782 to the young *studiosus philologiae et antiquitatum* Georg Zoëga, who had obtained a travelling scholarship to study ancient seals and coins with a view to re-arranging the Royal Collections. As will be remembered, it was Zoëga who elaborated the fundamental methods of Classical archaeology. In the first quarter of the 19th century Guldberg's collection, which, however, did not comprise any Classical sculptures, was bought by the King for his Art Cabinet; but some marbles, no doubt also earlier acquisitions including a fine posthumous portrait of the empress Livia (ABb 2), were transferred from the Royal Academy of Arts. A number of other sculptures brought to Denmark in the 18th century remained in private possession until modern economic development forced the owners to sell them. In this way two busts acquired by a Danish nobleman about 1780 and representing famous Greeks, the politician Hypereides and the philosopher Chrysippos, came to the National Museum in 1923 (8011 and 8012).

A new epoch was inaugurated in 1824 with the acquisition of a large Roman statue, probably intended to portray a lady belonging to the Imperial House; it was found in the North African town of Utica. The Danish consuls in Tunis, C.C. Holck and A.C. Gierlew, had been instrumental in bringing about this purchase as well as that of a portrait of Alexander the Great (ABb 1 and ABb 101). In 1821 the naval officer C.T. Falbe succeeded to their office, which resulted in a considerable increase of Danish scholarly interest in the antiquities of North Africa, whence several sculptures found their way to the museum in Copenhagen. Falbe was later transferred to Greece, where he remained from 1833 to 1835, to the great advantage of the Danish collections. From his return to Denmark to his death in 1849 he was attached to the private cabinet of antiquities of King Christian VIII. This collection contained several important sculptures, in addition to those procured by Falbe a number of marbles bought from the archbishop of Taranto, Giuseppe Capece Latro, among them two busts of Julio-Claudian princes and an altar, the reliefs of which alluded to Agrippa's victory at Actium (CVIII 305, CVIII 303 and CVIII 314); others were bought with the assistance of P.O. Brøndsted, the archaeologist, Chr. Hansen, the architect, and J.L. Ussing, the philologist. The same persons also helped to augment the Classical section of the Royal Museum of Art. The first acquisition of prehistoric Aegean sculpture to the latter took place in 1844, when two Cycladic figures (cat.Nos. 12 and 13) were transferred from the collection of Christian VIII, who a few years before had obtained them from the archaeologist Ludwig Ross. Similarly, the King in 1847 ceded a colossal head of Pan from the Athenian Acropolis, sent to him by Ussing (ABb 160). After the death of Christian VIII his entire cabinet of antiquities was in 1851 bought by the State. Among the important later acquisitions we must especially mention a series of large fragments from a public building at Pola in Istria embellished with sculptures (ABb 300-303), a small collection of marbles which had belonged to the Danish antiquarian Thomas Reutze in Vienna, i.a. a Lysippic Herakles head (ABb 294) and a portrait of the Egyptian king Ptolemy III (ABb 290), many items received through the agency of the artists J.A. Jerichau and T. Læssøe in Rome and the Danish consul J. Løytved in Beirut, and, last but not least, part of the material excavated by the Carlsberg Foundation's expeditions to Rhodes and Syria. A number of Etruscan works were purchased in the Italian art market.

In the second half of the 19th century, under the leadership of the archaeologists C.J. Thomsen, L. Müller and C. Blinkenberg, it was endeavoured to enlarge the collection, in order to convey to the visitor as comprehensive an impression of Classical art and civilization as possible; but in our century the Museum has desisted from systematic augmentation of its sculptural assemblage – a natural consequence of the creation of the Ny Carlsberg Glyptothek as a public museum in 1888.

Select bibliography:
P.J. Riis, Antiksamling i Danmark før Thorvaldsen, NMArb 1945, 54-60.
V. Hermansen, Fra Kunstkammer til Antik-Cabinet, Antik-Cabinettet 1851, Copenhagen 1951, 9-56,
N. Breitenstein, Christian VIII's Vasecabinet, ibid. 57-176.
Aa. Roussell (ed.), Danmarks Nationalmuseum, Copenhagen 1957.
M.-L. Buhl, A Hundred Masterpieces from the Ancient Near East in the National Museum of Denmark and the History of its Ancient Near Eastern Collections, Copenhagen 1974.
P.J. Riis, Klassisk og nærorientalsk arkæologi, Københavns Universitet 1479-1979 XI, Copenhagen 1979, 121-160.

AEGEAN SCULPTURES

That Trojan and Cycladic sculptures have here been placed under the same general heading is because the early West-Anatolian cultures are connected by several links with those of the Aegean sphere, just as Eastern Anatolia was oriented towards Mesopotamia, Syria and Iran. This holds especially true of the primitive works of art[1].

The majority of the Museum's prehistoric Aegean sculptures come from the Greek islands, but in 1885 Heinrich Schliemann presented four idols (Nos. 1-4) and a number of other objects excavated by himself at Troy[2]. The first acquisition of early Cycladic sculpture took place in 1844 when two figures from Thera and Ios were transferred from the private collection of King Christian VIII, who a few years before had obtained them from Ludwig Ross (Nos. 12 and 13). The later accessions are due to purchase by various Danish archaeologists travelling in Greece. Nearly all of the pieces acquired in this way were said to have been found on Amorgos (Nos. 5-6, 8, 9, 10 and 11). For one, however, the provenience is Keos (No. 14).

Nos. 1-14 allow us to follow the earliest sculptural development in those regions which later were to be populated by the Greeks. In all cases the material is marble, the original source of which unfortunately cannot yet be located more precisely[3], but for the most primitive-looking of the Trojan pieces, which seem to be pebbles casually picked up and roughly worked (Nos. 1-2), the sculptor obviously used the available local stone[4]. Both the Trojan and the most abstract of the Cycladic types (Nos. 1-6) are related to the Aegean Neolithic figures representing a squatting naked woman[5], whereas the appearance of the more developed Cycladic sculptures (Nos. 7-14) is possible due to Oriental influence[6].

Dates are given by similar sculptures found not only in Troy and on the Cyclades, but also in Crete and several other places, as will be set out in more detail below. On the other hand, some uncertainty still reigns as regards the interpretation of the figures[7], but one thing is clear, that they occur both in settlements and in cemeteries[8]. Certain graves contained sculptures that had had to be broken to be placed there[9], or which had been repaired, thus presumably implying use before burial. These facts seem to preclude the possibility that they were made exclusively for sepulchral purposes[10]. It is perhaps most reasonable to consider the female figures as images of a maternal fertility deity[11]. Sometimes pregnancy is indicated (No. 7)[12]. The figures of the most frequent Cycladic idol type cannot stand, but must lie on their backs, and could therefore represent a woman being delivered[13]. One might argue, however, that, since the double figure type representing a woman with her child on her head (No. 12), which must have been intended to stand, has the same "tip-toe" posture, then that posture is hardly to be taken as a criterion for the figure's position as lying. Moreover, there is a certain general likeness to Near-Eastern figures of the Naked Goddess[14].

TROY

Third and Beginning of Second Millennium B.C.

The Trojan sculptures (Nos. 1-4) belong to the category called "Brettidole"[15]. The specimens found during Schliemann's own excavations were regarded as having come from the deposits of Troy II-IV with a few exceptions from I and V[16]. For the dating of these layers we may refer to the fact that the later, American excavators found Early Helladic pottery in the deepest strata of Troy V and Gray Minyan Ware in its uppermost layers, so that this phase of the town's history must be placed about 2000 B.C.[17] The Americans also brought to light numerous idols, the shapes nearest to those of the specimens in the Danish National Museum being C. Blegen's types 1 B, 2 B and 3 E-F[18].

Among our idols only one has an appearance that renders the human form with any precision, a so-called "idol amulet" of "fiddle shape" (No. 4); a less clearly differentiated figure is shown by another "idol amulet" (No. 3), while two "amulet stones" (Nos. 1-2) are quite simple; their apparent primitivity might lead one to regard them as the earliest, were it not that excavations, not only at Troy, have shown that such types may occur alongside the more developed ones. The parallel material produced during the American investigations at Troy lay in contexts from I b to III b, except for stray finds in early VI. Type 1 was represented both in early Troy I and in II c and g, type 2 in early and middle I and in II g, type 3 in early I, II f and g; some specimens of type 2, however, also occurred in III a – b and in early VI. Troy I probably belonged to the first half of the 3rd millennium B.C., II to the third quarter and IV to the end of the same millennium[19]: but at Kusura in the region of Afyun Karahissar, in layer C, as well as in the necropolis of Yortan and in the deepest layer of the Protesilaos Mound at the Dardanelles, there were idols related to our Nos. 1-2, which may accordingly have been made at any time during the 3rd millennium and the beginning of the 2nd. Generally speaking the long-necked "fiddle shaped" idols are younger. Figures like our Nos. 3-4 were found by the Americans in Troy II f and g, but the Germans placed their counterparts in Troy IV-V, and similar specimens appeared in the transitional layer between Kusura B and C, i.e. at the end of the 3rd and the beginning of the 2nd millennium. The shape was developed from a simpler one in Troy I, a type which in Crete is found with Early Minoan I material[20].

1. Flat figure-of-eight "idol stone"

Produced by roughly cutting the longer edges of a flat oval pebble. Medium-grained white marble with greenish grey veins. H. 0.078 m.

Inv.No. 3000. Provenience: Hissarlik (Troy). Acquired 1885 from H. Schliemann. – NMFührer[3], Copenhagen 1908, 80 No. 5, NMVAntiksamlingen[3], Copenhagen 1918, 84 No. 5, AntK 8 1965, 82 note 44 pl. 23.8, NMArb 1970, 55 fig. 15, bottom left.
   Cp. Schmidt, SS, 277-278 Nos. 7347, 7355 and 7358, Dörpfeld, T&I I, 381 fig. 348 b, f and g, from Troy, Troy I, 112 fig. 216: 33.217, from Troy I b, Troy II, 69 fig. 48: 34.320, from Troy III b, Archaeologia 87 1937, 251 fig 17.2-3, 266, 268, from Kusura C, CRAI 1901, 814 pl. 1 centre and right, from Yortan. Related, but not flat idols: R. Demangel, Le tumulus dit de Protésilas, Paris 1926, 32, 28 fig. 31.20, 31 fig.35.4 and 9, 32 fig. 36, from the Protesilaos Mound, period I, AJA 75 1971, 135 pl. 29, from Aphrodisias. Near to Troy type 2 B.

2. Flat figure-of-eight "idol stone"

Resembling No. 1. Fine-grained greyish white marble. H. 0.071 m.

Inv.No. 3001. Provenience: Hissarlik (Troy). Acquired 1885 from H. Schliemann. – NMFührer[3], Copenhagen 1908, 80 No. 5, NMVAntiksamlingen[3], Copenhagen 1918, 84 No. 5, AntK 8 1965, 82 note 44 pl. 23.7, I. Strøm, Grækenlands forhistoriske kulturer I, Odense 1966, 104 fig. 95 right, NMArb 1970, 55 fig. 15, bottom right.
   Cp. Troy I, 112 fig. 216: 33.217, from Troy I b, 352 fig. 360: 35.208, from Troy II g, Troy II, 69 fig. 48: 34.429, from Troy III a, Troy III, 124 fig. 298: 37.334, from early Troy VI, AJA 71 1967, 253-254 pl. 77.15, from Karataş, AJA 75 1971, 135 pl. 29, from Aphrodisias. Intermediary between Troy types I B and 2 B.

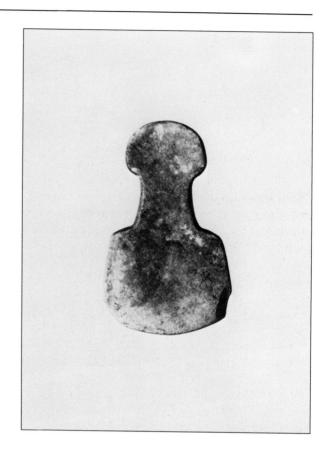

3. Flat figure-of-eight "idol amulet"

Head, neck and body clearly rendered, but not distinctly set off from one another. The body is broadest above. Both the flat sides and the edges are carefully cut. Coarse-grained light greyish marble. H. 0.071 m.

Inv.No. 2299. Provenience: Hissarlik (Troy). Acquired 1885 from H. Schliemann. – NMFührer[3], Copenhagen 1908, 80 No. 5, NMVAntiksamlingen[3], Copenhagen 1918, 84 No. 5, I. Strøm, Grækenlands forhistoriske kulturer I, Odense 1966, 104 fig. 95, left, NMArb 1970, 55 fig. 15, top right.
  Cp. Schmidt, SS, 278-279 Nos. 7363, 7461 and 7462, Dörpfeld, T&I I, 379 fig. 344 d-e, 382 fig. 349, IstForsch 6 1934, 37 pl. 16.13, from Troy, BMSculpture I 1, 3 A 1-2 pl. 1, from Namurt (Kyme), AJA 68 1964, 277 pl. 82.24, AJA 71 1967, 253-254 pl. 77.14, from Karataş. Quadrangular head and neck all in one, and offset shoulders, but otherwise resembling: Archaeologia 86 1936, 29 fig. 11.5, 50, from Kusura, "unstratified". Intermediary between Troy types 3 E and F, of Kusura type, AJA 73 1969, 4-5.

4. Flat figure-of-eight "idol amulet"

Head, neck and body clearly separated. Rounded contour of head, body broadest below. Both the flat sides and the edges are carefully cut. Fine-grained brown and white marble. H. 0.055 m.

Inv.No. 2298. Provenience: Hissarlik (Troy). Acquired 1885 from H. Schliemann. – NMFührer[3], Copenhagen 1908, 80 No. 5, NMVAntiksamlingen[3], Copenhagen 1918, 84 No. 5, NMArb 1970, 55 fig. 15, top left.
  Cp. Schmidt, SS, 279 Nos. 7461, 7462 and 7520, Dörpfeld, T&I I, 379 fig. 344 d-e and g, IstForsch 6 1934, 37 pl. 16.13, from Troy, Troy I, 310, 368 fig. 360: 36.34 and 37.469, from Troy II f and g, BMSculpture I 1, 3 A 1-2 pl. 1, from Namurt (Kyme), Archaeologia 86 1936, 251 fig. 17.4, 266, 268 pl. 84.11, from Kusura, "Early Transitional", AJA 68 1964, 277 pl. 82.24, AJA 71 1967, 253-254 pl. 77.14, from Karataş, H.T. Bossert, Alt-Anatolien, Berlin 1942, 23 No. 133 pl. 21, from the region of Magnesia. Near Troy type 3 F, of Kusura type, AJA 73 1969, 4-5.

THE CYCLADES

Late Fourth, Third and Beginning of Second Millennium B.C.

There is no doubt that the sculptures enumerated under this heading date from the early metallurgic cultures of the Cyclades. The nearest parallels have been found in graves and house-ruins attributed to the periods Early Cycladic I-III A[21], as well as in corresponding contexts in Crete and on the Greek Mainland.

The abstract idols Nos. 5-6 belong to the so-called Grotta-Pelos Culture, which takes its name from cemeteries on the islands of Naxos and Melos, and which has also left its traces in graves on Paros, Antiparos, Despotikon, Siphnos, Kimolos, Amorgos, Thera and Keos, probably of the time c. 3200/3000-2500 B.C., perhaps earlier[22]. Nos. 7-14 are figures ascribed to the subsequent Keros-Syros Culture, of which remains datable to c. 2500-1900 B.C. or earlier have been found particularly on Naxos, Paros, Antiparos, Amorgos, Syros, Melos, Thera and Keros[23].

It is the non-Cycladic, especially Cretan, finds[24] which can best be used to date the Museum's Cycladic figures. Some resembling Nos. 7-14 were brought to light in or near the tholos tombs at Koumasa[25] and at Platanos[26]. The tomb contents are quite predominantly Early Minoan I-III, but Middle Minoan I objects occur, particularly among the material from Tholos B at Platanos[27]. At Lebena in southern Crete other similar figures were lying together with Early Minoan II vessels, but in one case with Middle Minoan I A pottery[28]. On the other hand it is hardly realistic to maintain that an abstract figure on a Minoan seal from the Idaean Cave represents a fiddle-shaped idol of Cycladic type, as has indeed been proposed[29]; the seal is much later, from Late Minoan III A according to Sir Arthur Evans[30].

In Attica both primitive idols related to Nos. 5-6 and fragments of figures like Nos. 7-14 were found in Early Helladic II graves at Hagios Kosmas[31], and in Zygouriais near Corinth a fragment of a corresponding specimen was discovered before the American excavations and on the very spot where later the excavators' "Trench VI" was dug[32]; in this trench both Early and Middle Helladic material was brought to light[33]. Abstract figurines are also found in graves on Euboea, as well as "Folded Arms Figurines"[34].

Among the discoveries on the Cyclades it is particularly the objects from Phylakope on Melos which must be singled out as important for determining the lower limit; however, some doubt remains as to whether such figurines were made after Early Cycladic III A[35]. Fiddle-shaped idols (cf. Nos. 5-6) are published as coming from the excavation sectors K 2 and H 2, without further information[36], and from H 2 at a depth of 1.50-2.80 m.[37] The more developed type (cf. Nos. 7-14) is represented by fragments from B 5, a deposit immediately above bed-rock[38], and from H 3, at a depth of 2.00-3.00 m. together with painted pottery with geometric patterns found on a floor almost on bed-rock[39], and finally by a surface find[40].

Judging from both the Cretan and the Melian evidence, to which we must add newer material from Keos[41], we thus get the impression that some Cycladic sculptures of the categories here dealt with may still have remained in use at the beginning of the 2nd millennium B.C.[42], even if the majority were made in the 3rd millennium[43]. Of the finds from Hagia Eirene on Keos, however, only one of four marble figurines from the Early Cycladic strata comes from a firmly attested Early Cycladic II context[44], the rest, 38 fragments, are from Middle or even Late Bronze Age layers, or from surface finds. The five fragments from Late Bronze Age contexts may all have been reused as implements[45], which seems to suggest that their original function and/or symbolic significance was forgotten, though three of the fragments have been assigned by Schofield to a ritual context[46].

5. Flat "fiddle-shaped" idol

Head and neck are rendered as a long, pointed protuberance. The upper and lower parts of the body are separated by a notch in each of the lateral edges. There is furthermore a minor notch on each "shoulder". The lower edge is horizontal. Both the flat sides and the edges are carefully worked. On the lower edge sparse remains of red colour. Coarse-grained yellowish white marble. Polished. H. 0.036 m.

Inv.No. 4699. Provenience: Amorgos, together with Nos. 6, 8, 10 and 11 found in graves in the year 1894. Acquired 1896 from a dealer in Athens. – NMVAntik-samlingen[3], Copenhagen 1918, 87 No. 13, I. Strøm, Grækenlands forhistoriske kulturer I, Odense 1966, 123, 128 fig. 121, NMArb. 1989, 78, fig. 16.
   Cp. AEphem 1898, 159, 162 pl. 11.8 and 14, from Paros and Antiparos, BMSculpture I 1, 5-6, A 6-7 pl. 1, from Antiparos and Amorgos, Phylakopi 194 pl. 39.3-4, from Phylakope on Melos, AJA 73 1969, 4-5 I B fig. 1 pl. 2 d-e.

6. Flat "fiddle-shaped" idol

The neck is clearly separated from the body by means of two converging grooves on one of the flat sides. The upper and lower parts of the body are separated by a cut in each of the lateral edges. The lower part of the body tapers downward, but there is a nearly horizontal lower edge. The flat sides are carefully worked, the edges rounded. Coarse-grained yellowish white marble. On the lower edge and in the neck grooves remains of red colour. The upper end of the neck-and-head protuberance is missing. H. 0.071 m.

Inv.No. 4698. Provenience: Amorgos, together with Nos. 5, 8, 10 and 11 found in graves in the year 1894. Acquired 1896 from a dealer in Athens. NMVAntik-samlingen[3], Copenhagen 1918, 87 No. 13, I. Strøm, Grækenlands forhistoriske kulturer I, Odense 1966, 123, 128 fig. 121, NMArb. 1989, 78, fig. 16.
   Cp. AEphem 1898, 159, 162 pl. 11.4 and 8, from Paros and Antiparos, BMSculpture I 1, 5-6, A 7 pl. 1, from Amorgos, Phylakopi 194 pl. 39.7, from Phylakope on Melos, AJA 73 1969, 4-5, I B fig. 1, Hesperia 40 1971, 119-120 No. 29 pl. 22, from Hagia Eirene on Keos.

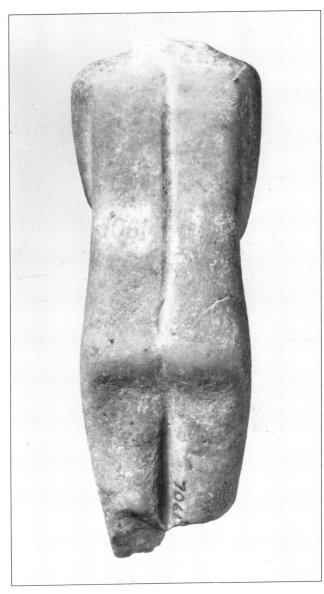

7. Naked woman

The trunk is comparatively flat, but the breasts are low, domed projections, the arms quite three-dimensional, and the abdomen slightly domed. Fingers are not indicated. There are slight traces of an incised triangle marking the pubic region and a vertical groove seemingly indicating the rima. On the back a deep dorsal groove. The buttocks are distinctly marked. The thighs seem slightly moved forwards. Medium-grained yellowish white marble with a light brownish yellow patina. The head, neck and legs from a little above the knees are missing. H. 0.139 m.

Inv.No. 7061. Provenience unknown. Acquired 1913 from a dealer in Athens. Instead of the original head another one of coarse-grained yellowish white to light ▷

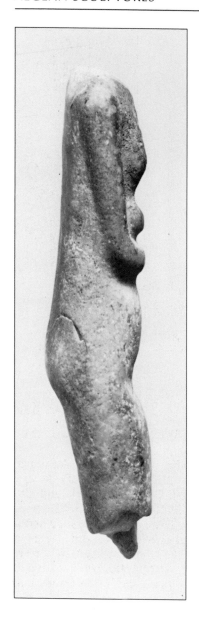

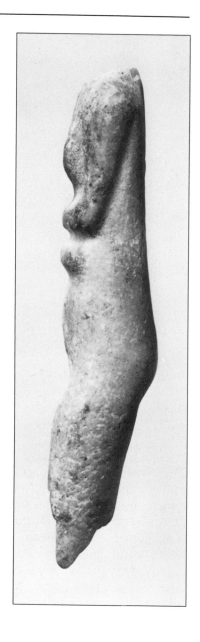

brownish marble was put in its place (No. 10a). NMArb. 1989, 75, fig. 11.

CP. AEphem 1898, 152 pl. 10.2, from Amorgos, BMSculpture I 1, 10, A 21 pl. 2, from Antiparos, Xanthoudides 22 No. 122 pls. 7 and 21, AJA 73 1969, 20 IV F 27 pl. 4 c, BSA 66 1971, 61, from Koumasa in Crete, V. Müller, Frühe Plastik in Griechenland und Vorderasien, Augsburg 1929, 9-10, 33, 168, 188 pl. 10.213-215, from Syros. The domed abdomen may possibly, but does not necessarily, mean pregnancy. About the latter there is no doubt in the cases of the Koumasa figure just referred to and of a specimen from Naxos, Compterendu du Congrès international d'Archéologie, Athens 1905, 222-223 with fig. Two figures of obviously pregnant women have also been found at Hagia Eirene on Keos, Hesperia 40 1971, 116 pl. 18.5-6, and for a similar figure of unknown provenience, see Thimme 274 cat. No. 183, and for another "from Attica", ibid. 275 cat. No. 185. Pregnant women are represented several times in the sculpture of the Keros-Syros Culture, AJA 73 1969, 11. Belongs to the so-called Kapsala group, which appears in the central Cyclades from Antiparos to Naxos and Amorgos, considered by Renfrew, AJA 73, 1969, 15-16, 21-22, to be the earliest group of figures in the Keros-Syros culture.

8. Naked woman

The head is rather flat, rectangular in shape at the top and elliptical below. At the back the head is not clearly offset from the neck, which, moreover, passes smoothly into the trunk. The arms are more three-dimensional that on Nos. 11-12 and 14, just as the trunk, the breasts and the legs have more natural proportions. Neither fingers nor toes have, however, been rendered. The pubic region is only indicated by means of the two inguinal furrows. There is a long dorsal groove unconnected with the separation of the legs, which is so deep as to produce an oval opening at the hams and calves. The knees are slightly bent. Fine-grained yellowish white marble. Polished. There are red dots on the cheeks and on the forehead below a shallow horizontal incision that possibly renders a diadem. Mouth and two necklaces are marked in red colour. H. 0.211 m.

Inv.No. 4695. Provenience: Amorgos, together with Nos. 5-6, 10 and 11 found in graves in the year 1894. Acquired 1896 from a dealer in Athens. – V. Poulsen, Från grottorna till Rom, Stockholm 1965, 106, I. Strøm, Grækenlands forhistoriske kulturer I, Odense 1966, 124, 129 fig. 122 a, G. Boesen, Danske Museumsskatte, Copenhagen 1967, 19 pl. 56 centre left, NMArb. 1989, 72, figs. 6 and 19.

Cp. AEphem 1898, 152 pl. 10.2, from Amorgos, BMSculpture I 1, 10, A 23-24 pl. 2 from Paros and Syros, Thimme 268, cat.No. 165, from Syros, and also the figure Xanthoudides, 22 No. 122 pls. 7 and 21, from Koumasa in Crete, which, however, has a domed abdomen probably indicating pregnancy. As for the traces of colour on forehead and cheeks, most likely indicating tattoo marks, see MémSocAntN 1896, 46-50. An awl of bronze with a handle of finely cut stone, bought in Athens 1887 and possibly from Amorgos, also held in the Danish National Museum, inv.No. 3263, was taken by C. Blinkenberg, Aarb 11 1896, 44 fig. 10, Mém-SocAntN 1896, 49 fig. 14, P. Fossing, NMVAntiksamlingen[4], Copenhagen 1935, 29 No. 58, and I.Strøm, op. cit. 123, 127 fig. 119, to have been used for tattooing. Another similar awl has been found in the much disputed Tomb D at Kapros on Amorgos, of Early Cycladic date, AJA 71 1967, 18 pl. 4.20-21, K. Branigan, Aegean Metalwork of the Early and Middle Bronze Age, Oxford 1974, 199 No. 3354, Thimme 570-573. The figure belongs to the so-called Spedos Group that is particularly known from Naxos, but otherwise widely spread, even to Crete and the Greek mainland. The Spedos Group is the most common of all and seems to have appeared a little earlier than the Dokathismata Group, but, broadly speaking, it is contemporary with it, AJA 73 1969, 22, 28 fig. 4.

9. Naked woman

Head, neck, trunk and limbs are all rather flat. The outline of the head is trapezoidal above, elliptical below. The neck is distinctly set off from both head and trunk by means of a groove. The breasts are low projections. The arms are but slightly three-dimensional, all fingers are rendered, but of equal length. The upper border of the pubic region is marked by a horizontal groove, the rima by a verti-cal one, the inguinal furrows are curved. On the back there is a dorsal groove unconnected with the separation of the legs, which is very deep, both on the front and the back. Coarse-grained yellowish white marble, in places with a brownish patina. On the front lime incrustations. The legs are missing from the knees downward. H. 0.496 m.

▷

Inv.No. 1624. Provenience: Amorgos. Acquired 1881 from a dealer in Athens. – Den kgl. Antiksamling, Haandkatalog[4], Copenhagen 1884, 32 No. 63, Aarb 11 1896, 8 fig. 1, 9 No. 1 a, 57 (Amorgos Z), MémSocAntN 1896, 7 No. 1a, fig. 1, 62 (Amorgos Z), S. Müller, De forhistoriske Tider i Europa, Copenhagen 1904, 20 fig. 23, S. Müller, Den förhistoriska tiden i Europa, Stockholm 1905, 26 fig. 23, S. Müller, Urgeschichte Europas, Strassburg 1905, 33 fig. 23, S. Müller, L'Europe préhis-

torique, Paris 1907, 35 fig. 23, D. Fimmen, Die kretisch-mykenische Kultur, Leipzig & Berlin 1921, 14, Aarsti-derne 2, Copenhagen 1943, 100 with fig., V. Poulsen, Skulpturbogen I, Stockholm 1947, pl. 16, NMVAntik-samlingen[5], Copenhagen 1948, 47 No. 2 pl. 11 left, Guides to the National Museum, Department of Orien-tal and Classical Antiquities, Copenhagen 1950, 48 No. 2 pl. 11 left, Early Art in Greece, the Cycladic, Minoan, Mycenean and Geometric Periods 3000-700 B.C., Odense 1965, 14 No. 23, G. Boesen, Danske Museums-skatte, Copenhagen 1967, 19 pl. 56 left, NMVAntik-samlingen, Grækenland, Italien og Romerriget, Copenhagen 1968, 14-15 with fig. right, 25 No. 2, Guides to the National Museum, Greece, Italy and the Roman Empire, Copenhagen 1968, 14-15 with fig. right, 25 No. 2, AJA 73 1969, 20 IV F 18 pl. 4 b, J. Bender & B. Bundgaard Rasmussen, Oldtidens Grækenland, Copenhagen 1981, 12 fig. 1, P. Getz-Preziosi, in Cyc-ladiaca 49 fig. 5 c, 6 c, 7 c, idem, Sculptors of the Cyc-lades, Individual and Tradition in the Third Mille-nium B.C., Ann Arbor 1987, 88 pl. 24,3, 157, namepiece for the Copenhagen Master, NMArb. 1989, 68, fig. 1.

Cp. BMSculpture I 1, 9, A 18 fig. 7, from Amorgos. Probably belonging to the Spedos Group, see above ad No. 8.

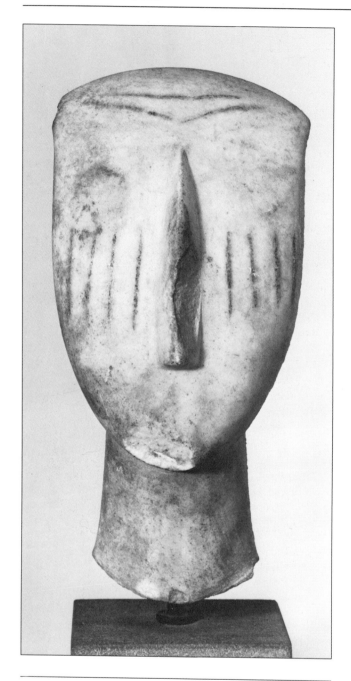

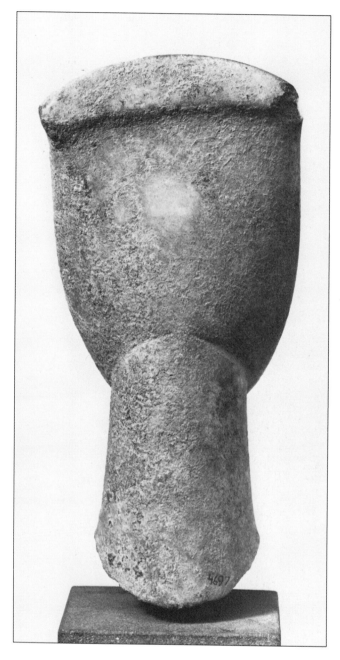

10. Head and neck of figure of naked woman

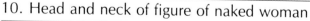

The outline is nearly rectangular at the top, elliptical below. Coarse-grained yellowish white marble. On the forehead transversal red stripes as well as traces of black paint. Remains of black paint also indicate the outline of the eyes. On the cheeks and the nose vertical red stripes. On the neck indefinite traces of both red and black paint. Fracture surface below. Part of nose and part of chin are missing. H. 0.246 m.

Inv.No. 4697. Provenience: Amorgos, together with Nos. 5-6, 8 and 11 found in graves in the year 1894. Acquired 1896 from a dealer in Athens. – NMFührer[3]. Copenhagen 1908, 82-83 No. 14, NMAntiksamlingen[3], Copenhagen 1918, 87 No. 14, K. Friis Johansen (ed.), De forhistoriske Tider i Europa I, Copenhagen 1927, 140 fig. 68, NMVAntiksamlingen[4], Copenhagen 1935, 27, 29 No. 58, Aarstiderne 2, Copenhagen 1943, 99 with fig., 101, A. Bruhn & L. Hjortsø, Klassisk Kunst I & III, Copenhagen 1945, fig. 40 right, NMVAntiksamlingen[5], Copenhagen 1948, 47 No. 2 pl. 11 upper right, Guides to the National Museum, Department of Oriental and

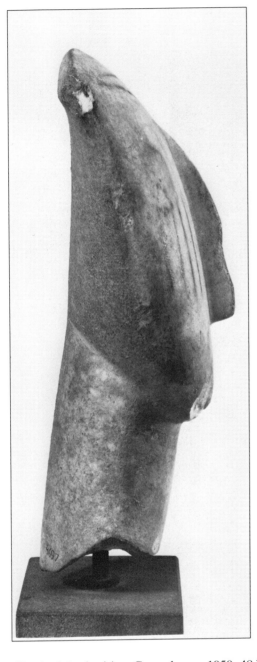

439 pl. 32.1, Kunst und Kultur der Kykladen im Jahr 3000 vor Christus, ed. J. Thimme, Karlsruhe 1976, 466 pl. 5, C. Doumas, Art des Cyclades, Collection N.P. Goulandris, 77 no. 44bis, P. Getz-Preziosi, Sculptors of the Cyclades, Individual and Tradition in the Third Millenium B.C., Ann Arbor 1987, 100 pl. VII, 159, NMArb. 1989, 73, fig. 8.

Probably to be ascribed to the same type as Nos. 8-9. For the shape of the head and the traces of colour, partially rendering tattoo marks, see No. 8. C. Renfrew, AJA 73 1969, loc.cit., takes the stripes over the nose to be possibly the rendering of the eyebrows or of a diadem. The paint on the neck is perhaps what remains of the rendering of a necklace. The entire length of the figure was almost 1 m, if we calculate from the proportions of Nos. 8 and 11. The head thus belongs to the class of very large figures, C. Zervos, L'art des Cyclades, Paris 1957, figs. 160, 162, 178, 296 and 297. They may perhaps be regarded as cult images representing deities, AntK 8 1965, 78 No. 1, 79, C. Renfrew, in Cycladiaca 29.

Classical Antiquities, Copenhagen 1950, 48 No. 2 pl. 11, upper right, V. Poulsen, Från grottorna till Rom, Stockholm 1965, 106, I. Strøm, Grækenlands forhistoriske kulturer I, Odense 1966, 123, 127 fig. 120, G. Boesen, Danske Museumsskatte, Copenhagen 1967, 19 pl. 56 centre right, NMVAntiksamlingen, Grækenland, Italien og Romerriget, Copenhagen 1968, 14-15 with fig., centre, 25 No. 2, Guides to the National Museum, Greece, Italy and the Roman Empire, Copenhagen 1968, 14-15 with fig., centre, 25 No. 2, AJA 73 1969, 23 pl. 8 a, AntK 13 1970, 8 notes 19-20, 9 note 30, C. Renfrew, The Emergence of Civilisation, London 1972,

10a. Head and neck of figure of naked woman

The head has a nearly triangular outline and on the back the neck is not distinctly offset. The upper right corner of the head is missing. H. 0.047 m.

Inv.No. 7061a. Provenience unknown. Acquired 1913 from a dealer in Athens. At the time of acquisition it was joined to the body of No. 7. Originally the head must have belonged to a figure of the Spedos type. – NMArb. 1989, 75, fig. 12.

11. Naked woman

The head is flat, nearly trapezoidal and without details except a vertical rib indicating the nose. The neck is separated from head and trunk by means of a groove. The breasts are rendered in very low relief. The arms are merely marked by incisions, the lower arms held horizontally covering the diaphragm, the left above the right, fingers are not indicated. The pubic region is marked by means of an incised triangle. A long dorsal groove is indicated. Both the trunk and the legs are comparatively flat. The feet are stretched downwards, toes are indicated by incisions. Coarse-grained yellowish white marble. On the surface many marks of a tool with which the surface has been worked, or simply traces of abrasion. The legs have been broken at the knees, but are repaired. The toes of the right foot are missing. Also minor damage on the upper angles of the head. H. 0.300 m.

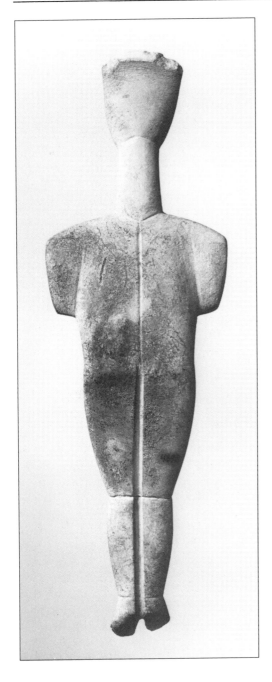

Inv.No. 4696. Provenience: Amorgos, together with Nos. 5-6, 8 and 10 found in graves in the year 1894. Acquired 1896 from a dealer in Athens. – NMVAntiksamlingen[4], Copenhagen 1935, 29 No. 58 with fig., K. Friis Johansen (ed.), De forhistoriske Tider i Europa I, Copenhagen 1927, 141 fig. 72, K. Birket-Smith, Kulturens Veje II, Copenhagen 1942, 36 fig. 6, A. Bruhn & L. Hjortsø, Klassisk Kunst I & III, Copenhagen 1945, fig. 40 left, NMVAntiksamlingen[5], Copenhagen 1948, 47 No. 2 pl. 11 lower right, Guides to the National Museum, Department of Oriental and Classical Antiquities, Copenhagen 1950, 48 No. 2 pl. 11 lower right, Antik-Cabinettet 1851, Copenhagen 1951, 128, NMVAntiksamlingen[6], Copenhagen 1955, 45 No. 2 pl. 12, K. Birket-Smith, Kulturens Veje[2] II, Copenhagen 1967, 155, G. Boesen, Danske Museumsskatte, Copenhagen 1967, 19 pl. 56 right, NMVGrækenland, Italien og Romerriget, Copenhagen 1968, 14-15 with fig. left, 25 No. 2, Guides to the National Museum, Greece, Italy and the Roman Empire, Copenhagen 1968, 14-15 with fig. left, 25 No. 2, NMArb. 1989, 73, figs. 7 and 19.

Cp. BMSculpture I 1, 8, A 15-16 fig. 5. pl. 2, "from Greece", ADelt 17 1961/2, 114-115 pl. 46 a-b, from grave 10 at Spedos on Naxos, Xanthoudides 22 No. 123 pl. 21, AJA 73 1969, 19 IV 1, BSA 66 1971, 63, from Koumasa in Crete, A. Evans, Cretan Pictographs, London & New York 1895, 124, 127-128 fig. 133, AJA 73 1969, 19 note 65, BSA 66 1971, 61, from Siteia in Crete, Hesperia 40 1971, 115 No. 2 pl. 17, from Hagia Eirene on Keos. Belongs to the so-called Dokathismata Group represented on several of the Cyclades, from Syros in the north to Melos in the south, AJA 73 1969, 12-13, 16-17. For tool marks, see E. Oustinoff in Cycladiaca, 42, cf. also, for example, the "Goulandris Queen", C. Doumas, Cycladic Art, Ancient Sculpture and Ceramics in the N.P. Goulandris Collection, Washington, D.C. 1979, 94-95, cat.No. 133.

12. Naked woman who originally carried a child on her head

The head is flat and nearly triangular. The neck is at the front set off from the trunk by means of a groove. The breasts are rendered as slight, domed projections. The arms are marked almost solely by incisions. The lower arms are held horizontally before the diaphragm, the left above the right. The fingers are not indicated. Trunk and legs are comparatively flat, but the abdomen is slightly domed. The pubic region is marked by an incised triangle. A dorsal groove continues into the separation of the legs, and the buttocks are distinct. Toes are not indicated. Only a small part of the legs of the child carried on the head is preserved. Coarse-grained greyish white marble. The legs have been broken at the middle of the thighs, but have been put together again. The right foot and a fragment of the front part of the right thigh are missing, in addition

to the greater part of the child. The surface is much weathered, especially on the face. H. 0.221 m.

Inv.No. ABb 139. Provenience: Ios. Acquired 1844 from King Christian VIII, who had obtained it from Ludwig Ross. – Det. kgl. Nordiske Oldskrift-Selskab, Aarsberetning, Copenhagen 1838, 14, S. Birket-Smith, Veiledning i Antikkabinettet[2], Copenhagen 1864, 17 No. 40 b, Compte-rendu du Congrès international d'Anthropologie et d'Archéologie préhistorique, Copenhagen 1869, 486 (the provenience erroneously gi-

ven as "Thera"), Aarb 11 1896, 9 fig. 3, 16 No. 6, 57 (Ios C), MémSocAntN 1896, 8 fig. 3, 16 No. 6, 64 (Ios C), D. Fimmen, Die kretisch-mykenische Kultur, Leipzig & Berlin 1921, 14, Antik-Cabinettet 1851, Copenhagen 1951, 128, AntK 8 1965, 78 note 24, AJA 73 1969, 14, 17 IV B 15 pl. 9 c, NMArb. 1989, 71, fig. 2.

Belongs to the same style group as No. 11. For the modelling of the abdomen, cp. No. 7. Female figures with a child on the head: Possibly the earliest and largest specimen depicting a definitely pregnant woman with a child on her head is in a private collection, but the provenience is not indicated, see P. Getz-Preziosi, Early Cycladic Sculpture, an Introduction, Malibu 1985, 15 pl. 3. – From Paros comes the specimen Thimme 303, 492-93, cat.No. 257; for another previously in a private collection in Zürich, now lost, see Thimme 44 fig. 24. There are furthermore a fragmentary figure in the Goulandris Collection in Athens, unpublished, and possibly two fragmentary figures from Tenos and Cape Krio (Asia Minor), JHS 9 1888, 82, AntK 8 1965, 78 note 24.

13. Naked woman

The head has a triangular outline; at the back it is not distinctly offset from the neck, which however is separated from the shoulders by means of a groove on both sides. The breasts are rendered as low domed projections. Arms and a roll of flesh above them are rendered by incisions. A dorsal groove continues into the separation of the legs, which is also only a groove. Coarse-grained greyish white marble. The lower parts of the legs are missing. The surface somewhat weathered. H. 0.154 m.

Inv.No. ABb 139. Provenience: Thera. Acquired 1844

from King Christian VIII, who obtained it from Ludwig Ross, cf. the latter's remarks in Reisen auf den griechischen Inseln I, Stuttgart & Tübingen 1840, 181, on the acqusition in Megalochorion on Thera 1837 of "einige jener alterthümlichen Marmorfigürchen, nebst Pfeilspitzen aus Obsidian, die zusammen in Gräbern gefunden worden waren". – Det kgl. Nordiske Oldskrift-Selskab, Aarsberetning, Copenhagen 1838, 14, S. Birket-Smith, Veiledning i Antikkabinettet[2], Copenhagen 1864, 17 No. 40 b, Compte-rendu du Congrès international d'Anthropologie et d'Archéologie préhistorique, Copenhagen 1869, 486, SBWien 73 1873, 239-240, Aarb 11 1896, 9 No. 1 a, 61 (Thera C), MémSocAntN 1896, 7 No. 1 a, 67 (Thera C), Thera II, Berlin 1903, 138 note 12, CVA Copenhague, Musée National 2, II B, 47 ad pl.

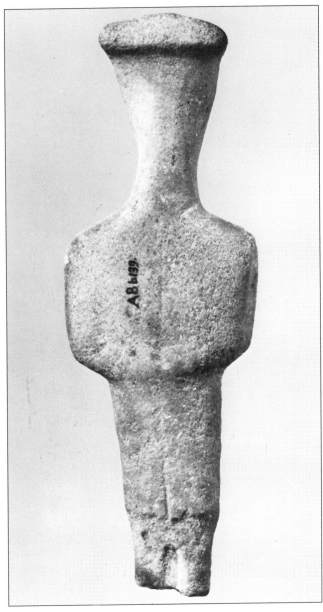

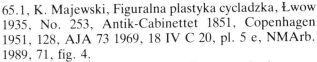

65.1, K. Majewski, Figuralna plastyka cycladzka, Łwow 1935, No. 253, Antik-Cabinettet 1851, Copenhagen 1951, 128, AJA 73 1969, 18 IV C 20, pl. 5 e, NMArb. 1989, 71, fig. 4.

The information that this figure and the vase CVACopenhague, Musée National 2, II B pl. 65.1 both come from Thera has by some scholars been taken to mean that they belonged to the contents of the same grave. The vase, which in 1838 was given by Ross to Christian VIII, then a prince, and which was not transferred to the Museum until 1851, had probably been excavated by Ross in the Sellada necropolis on Thera in 1835, cf. Reisen auf den griechichen Inseln I, 66, Thera I, Berlin 1899, 20. For parallels to No. 13, see Thimme 289, 480, cat.No. 227, provenience unknown. It belongs to the so-called Chalandriani Group, named after a locality on Syros, though also represented on others of the Cyclades, e.g. Keos, Naxos and Paros. Rolls of flesh are generally taken as indicative of the so-called Keos Group, AJA 73 1969, 18, but are also found on figures of the Chalandriani Group, Thimme 287, 289, cat.Nos. 222, 230-231; on the known examples the rolls of flesh are, however, rendered below the arms. C. Renfrew, AJA 73 1969, 22, regards the Chalandriani Group as roughly contemporary with the Koumasa Group, but partially later, cf. ibid. 28 fig. 4.

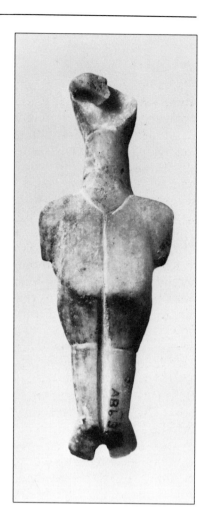

14. Naked woman

The head is nearly triangular. The breasts are slightly indicated. The neck is separated from the body by a semicircular groove. A dorsal groove continues into the separation of the legs. The hams are indicated by means of a horizontal groove. The toes are rendered by incisions. Coarse-grained yellowish white marble, in places with a light brown patina. The upper and back parts of the head are broken off; a small fragment has been put back into its old place, but the other pieces are missing. H. 0.099 m.

Inv.No. ABb 320. Provenience: Keos. Acquired 1865 from Jean Pio, the philologist, who had obtained it in Greece. Aarb 11 1896, 9 fig. 2, 10 No. 1 b, 58 (Keos A), MémSocAntN 1896, 8 No. 1 b fig. 2, 64 (Keos A), D. Fimmen, Die kretisch-mykenische Kultur, Leipzig & Berlin 1921, 14, C. Zervos, L'art des Cyclades, Paris 1957, 43, 270 note 284, NMArb. 1989, 72, fig. 5.

Cp. A. Evans, Cretan Pictographs, London & New York 1895, 124, 127-128 fig. 134, AJA 73 1969, 19 IV E 11, BSA 66 1971, 63, from Siteia in Crete, AA 1933, 298-302 fig. 9.2-3, AJA 73 1969, 19 IV E 8-9 pl. 6 c-d, BSA 66 1971, 63, from Teké in Crete. Related to the so-called Koumasa Group, which otherwise is limited to Crete, the specimens probably being Cretan imitations of Cycladic work. They are later than the Dokathismata Group and seem to be contemporary with Early Minoan II-III and perhaps Middle Minoan I, AJA 73 1969, 21-22, BSA 66 1971, 61-63 and 75 fig. 2.

CYPRIOTE SCULPTURES

The majority of the Cypriote sculptures have been found on the island of Rhodes during the Danish excavations of 1901-14, directed by K.F. Kinch and C. Blinkenberg. A few others associated with them were bought by Kinch, probably on Rhodes (Nos. 20, 29, 52 and 55); but only for one of these is the finding-place known, viz. Kalathos (No. 52). The sculptures from Cyprus proper are very few. Some specimens (Nos. 72, 78-80, 82 and 83) were received as early as 1853, as a gift from Henry Christy, the English ethnologist; they were found at Kition (Larnaka), like the objects which he presented to the British Museum[47]. Others were bought in Paris without further indication of provenience than "Cyprus". From the Asiatic mainland, however, there are also some pieces. Two heads were acquired in Syria 1880 and 1901 from Julius Løytved, the Danish vice-consul in Beirut[48]; one (No. 70), formerly in the Péretié Collection at Beirut, had been found at Marathos (ᶜAmrīt), the other (No. 57) was said to have come from Palmyra. The latter statement is evidently erroneous and is no doubt due to the specimen belonging to a series of small limestone heads, mostly Palmyrene, of which Løytved was then in possession; but it may well be a Syrian find like the other objects received from him in those years, and there is reason to believe that the provenience is Tripolis (Ṭarābulus) or its surroundings, as it was acquired together with an object found there. Finally, there are some heads from the neighbourhood of Ioppe (Yāfā), given to the Museum in 1883 by Valdemar Lausen, M.D. (Nos. 60, 71, 75, 76 and 81).

All the sculptures in this section are made of a light-coloured soft limestone (the Greek poros). Limestone figures of the types represented and brought to light in Rhodian excavations have been regarded as local products, although made under Cypriote influence[49]. It has been maintained that the material of the sculptures discovered at Kameiros is more "gritty" than that of the indisputable Cypriote pieces, furthermore that the kouros type was frequent on Rhodes, but seems to have been avoided in Cyprus, and finally that the Rhodian lion-fighter type is not identical with the Cypriote one, but similar to that occurring at Naukratis in Egypt. Moreover, it has seemed that there were no Cypriote counterparts to several other types, at the best Naukratite ones, and this was taken to hold true particularly of the seated lions and the falcons. Blinkenberg, on the other hand, thought that one should not hesitate to accept the idea of a Cypriote origin, and he explained the apparently non-Cypriote types as produced or selected in Cyprus especially for export[50].

In the later years the situation has changed, and Lone Wriedt Sørensen is probably right in taking the finds to mean that Greek import of Cypriote sculpture took place while at the same time there existed in certain towns sculptural workshops established by immigrant Cypriots, at least at Naukratis[51]. To judge from the discoveries in Phoenicia, we have also there to reckon with both import from Cyprus and a local production of objects in Cypriote style, either by Cypriots or by Phoenicians copying Cypriote models[52]; there is, for instance, an obvious difference between the stone that was normally used at Sūkās and which is local, and the material of the better sculptures from there and from Marathos (ᶜAmrīt) (e.g. No. 70), which is probably of Cypriote origin.

Generally speaking, the limestone of which the Museum's Rhodian pieces have been made is a fine-grained variety, the surface of which weathers with numerous tiny pits of the size of a prick with a needle, which gives the stone, seen through a magnifying-glass, a pock-marked appearance; the stone is white in the core, light yellowish-grey to light brownish on the surface. The very same material has also been employed for several, perhaps all, of the heads found near Ioppe, and for No. 77, which is certainly Cypriote, as well as for certain fragments in the Ny Carlsberg Glyptotek of non-Rhodian provenience[53]. Quite different is the stone of the National Museum's heads from Kition and other specimens found in Cyprus; it is coarser and white with an uneven light greyish, not yellowish surface without the above-mentioned pits, but not infrequently containing obvious fossils[54]. Finally, there are a few, Nos. 57 and 22, from Syria (Tripolis?) and Lindos respectively, that have darker particles in the white core and a yellowish brown surface; Phoenician work is excluded, if for no other reason, by the fact of the stone differing from the local varieties. Of course, these differences of material imply the use of different quarries or parts of quarries, but to judge from the proveniences there is no obstacle to supposing that the quarries from which the Museum's Cypriote sculptures came were actually situated in Cyprus. It is true that Kinch[55] gave the information that a fine uniform poros occurred naturally both on Rhodes and in Cyprus; but this is a remark of a general character, and comparison of the sculptures in question with an indisputable sample of Rhodian poros, also kept in Copenhagen, shows the latter to have another, quite distinctive look[56]. Finally, it should be mentioned that our Nos. 57, 59 and 72, from Syria (Tripolis?), Lindos and Kition respectively, have been petrographically examined by Dr. Poul Graff-Petersen, departmental head in the University Museum of Geology, Copenhagen, and according to him – and in spite of the above-mentioned differences – the material is the same in all three cases, which corroborates the theory of export from Cyprus.

Among the statuary types represented in the Museum's Cypriote series particularly the lions (Nos. 23-30), the falcons (Nos. 35-41), certain sphinxes (Nos. 32-34) and seated figures (Nos. 21, 61-66) may formerly have aroused antagonism in being labelled "Cypriote". However, lions like those found on Rhodes, but occurring at Naukratis, are made of local *sand*stone[57], while in Cyprus they are of *lime*stone[58]. Closely related lions are to be seen on a tomb-stone from Amathous, but there they are cruder and turn their heads in conformity with the rules of decoration[59], while the same posture as the Lindian lions is found in a later specimen from Bounoi (Vouni)[60]. Moreover, recent publications have testified to the occurrence of the same lion types on Rhodes and in Cyprus[61]. Nor is the seated sphinx unknown in the Archaic Cypriote repertoire[62], just as there are representations from later periods[63]. The seated persons with a casket on their laps and those who only rest their hands on the arms of the chair may be compared with statuettes found in a 5th century grave at Marion[64]; for No. 64 there are Archaic Cypriote counterparts in terracotta. Even the falcons are exemplified in Cyprus[65]; but otherwise their nearest relatives are faience figures particularly manufactured at Naukratis[66]. It holds true of the falcons from Broulia (Vroulia) and Lindos[67], and of several of the other types as well, that it is easier to understand them as made in a Phoenicianized milieu than in a real Greek one. In Cyprus the sculptural finds having the purest Greek character were those at Marion, whereas the specimens excavated at Paphos, Amathous and Kition (cf. Nos. 72-74, 78-80, 82-83) display more mixed style features[68]. Some of the types, for example the lions, seem to have been put into production especially by workshops in the Salamis region and diffused from there[69].

To-day it seems most reasonable to conclude that the limestone figures dealt with here were manufactured in Cyprus; but some of them may have been made exclusively to meet the special demands of some foreign market, just as for instance was the case with the Tyrrhenian Amphorae. In this connection it must be pointed out that according to a recent investigation there may have been a small settlement of Phoenicians in Ialysos on Rhodes from the late 8th century B.C. until well into the 6th[70]. The Rhodian inscriptions on some of the sculptures do not contradict the idea of import, for corresponding Cypriote, Knidian and Ionian inscriptions occur[71]. The supposition of Cypriote sculptors working at Naukratis and on the Phoenician coast is acceptable in so far as the style of some pieces has a Cypriote look, but the stone is local. Cypriote graffiti have been found on pottery found at Naukratis[72]. and there is a literary tradition testifying to the dedication of a Cypriote sculpture in Naukratis[73].

As far as the distribution of Cypriote sculpture is concerned, some remarks may be added to Blinkenberg's survey[74]. The Italian finds at Kameiros have later been published[75], the figures from the Knidian peninsula likewise[76]. In addition to the Cypriote sculptures from Delos there are now several examples from Chios and Samos[77]. More problematical finding-places, although not to be excluded, are "one of the Greek islands" and "Melos"[78]. Among the pieces published by E. Renan one is from Antarados (Ṭarṭūs)[79]; he also mentioned a large discovery at Marathos (ᶜAmrīt)[80], to which presumably our No. 70 belongs, and which has been supplemented by the later finding of numerous other statuettes at the same place[81]. From the ancient capital of this part of Phoenicia, the island-city of Arados (Ar-Rūʾād), comes a specimen in London[82]. Other North Phoenician proveniences are Sūkās, Rās Ibn Hānī and Al-Mīna at the mouth of the Orontes[83]. A couple of Cypriote heads come from Byblos (Ǧubail)[84], and some pieces have been found at Sidon (Ṣaida)[85]. As was mentioned above, the Ioppe (Yāfā) region was the provenience of Nos. 60, 71, 75, 76 and 81, and to them we must now add some finds from the South-Palestinian coastland[86]. Finally, it seems that a head found in Lycia is also Cypriote[87].

A safe dating of the National Museum's Cypriote limestone figures is best afforded by the results of the excavations in Naukratis, Rhodes and Samos, as well as, of, course, those obtained by the Swedish Cyprus Expedition. In Naukratis[88] there were in the fill layers in the sanctuary of Apollon[89] fragments of several statuettes similar to those of the Museum[90]; they came from "Level 260"[91], below which stratum there was pottery from the second half of the 7th century B.C.[92], whereas the layer superimposed on "Level 260" contained sherds of the late 7th and the first half of the 6th century B.C. The Aphrodite sanctuary likewise had such ex-votos[93], and the building to which they must be ascribed is the first temple, which was founded in the second half of the 7th century at the earliest, most likely in the first half of the 6th[94]. This structure was probably destroyed in 525 B.C., when the Persians conquered Egypt; its successor is held to date from the end of the same century[95].

The settlement in Rhodes known under the modern name of Broulia (Vroulia) existed for nearly a hundred years until 570/560 B.C.[96]. In the so-called chapel, where the limestone figures were found, there was also pottery from the last quarter of the 7th century and the first quarter of the 6th[97]. With one exception the Lindos figures[98] were found in part in the Archaic terrace fill, in part in the bigger votive deposit, where they belonged to the so-called category B, in actual fact a remainder of the terrace layers. The lower chronological limit for the latter is fixed by two terracottas[99], of which the first one is roughly contemporary with Samian figures from c. 525 B.C.[100]; similar figures have turned up sporadically at Kameiros and at Megara Hyblaia[101]. The Lindos figures taken as a whole still have an Orientalizing character[102]. Cyprus was politically independent from 669 to c. 570 B.C.,

when the island came under Egyptian domination; Egyptian influence is traceable, however, already in the late 7th century[103], but the Greek impact was strongest under the Persians, i.e. after c. 545 B.C.[104]. Our No. 66, from Lindos, corresponds to a Cypriote figure found in the Harbour Cemetery at Sūkās, which apparently belonged to a grave of the period c. 550-500 B.C.[105]

It is possible to follow and give relative dates to the stylistic development on a basis of the finds in Cyprus itself, especially at Arsos, Kition, Bounoi (Vouni), Soloi, Hagia Eirene, and Mersinaki[106], but none of the limestone figures brought to light by excavations in that island, or on Samos or Chios[107], can be pushed farther back than to the later part of the 7th century B.C. According to some scholars this time limit should be placed c. 600 B.C.[108]; but in fact the earliest sculptures of the style represented in Broulia and Lindos occurred in Chios in a late 7th century context[109]. In the Samian Heraion there was, in a layer belonging to the time before Rhoikos' construction activity in the years 560/550 B.C., a lion figure resembling our Nos. 27 and 30, and in the ashes belonging to Rhoikos' altar, i.e. after 550, figures corresponding to Nos. 35-38, 41, 42 and 48[110]. It is therefore justifiable to reject all attempts at a higher chronology[111].

In conclusion we divide our Cypriote series into the following six style periods: (1) Nos. 15-41, Early Archaic, c. 625-565 B.C., (2) Nos. 42-69, Mature Archaic, c. 565-525 B.C., (3) Nos. 70-74, Late Archaic, c. 525-475 B.C., (4) Nos. 75-76 Early Classical, c. 475-400 B.C., (5) Nos. 77-79, Late Classical, 4th century B.C., and (6) Nos. 80-84, Hellenistic, 3rd to 1st centuries B.C.

The great majority of the Cypriote sculptures in the Danish National Museum were ex-votos; the Broulia, Lindos and Marathos finds were all made in sanctuaries. None of the figures or fragments enumerated is known with certainty to have been sepulchral, but the possibility exists at least in the case of No. 74.

EARLY ARCHAIC

C. 625-565 B.C.

Most of the Early Archaic representations of human beings belong to a stage of development corresponding to that of Eastern Greek productions, such as a couple of early bronzes from the Samian Heraion[112] (Nos. 15-17, 19, 20 and 22, cf. the faces of the sphinxes Nos. 32 and 33). The features of No. 21, on the other hand, may rather be compared with somewhat later works inspired from Ionia[113], just as the motif of the fragment recalls the earlier Ionian seated figures[114]. No. 21 is on the boundary to the Mature Archaic series, within which Nos. 46 and 53-55, with somewhat rounder and plumper faces, are its nearest relatives. As to the place which the lions Nos. 23-31 occupy in the stylistic development, it must be emphasized that some of those found in Cyprus[115] look a little earlier, as the modelling is less differentiated[116]. Presumably Nos. 23-31 should be placed nearer to 625 B.C. than to 565 B.C., and we should not forget that on Chios the lion type was represented in a late 7th century context.

15. Standing beardless man playing the double flute (auloi)

The hair is hanging in a broad mass down the nape; it seems to have been terminated horizontally at the shoulders. A groove at the neck indicates the rim of a dress. White limestone with light yellowish patina. Slight traces of red colour on the mouth, the cheeks and the mouth-piece of the flutes; the colouring probably represents the mouth-band (phorbeia). The left upper arm, the lower part of the figure and most of the back are missing. The surface somewhat scratched. H. 0.094 m.

Inv.No. 11327. Provenience: Broulia (Vroulia), so-called chapel. Acquired 1942 from the Carlsberg Foundation. – Vroulia 11, 15-16 No. 2 pls. 13.3 and 14.3, Lindos I, 402, 426. Kypern, fra stenalder til romertid, Ny Carlsberg Glyptotek, Copenhagen 1983, 61 No. 164.

Similar flute-players are known from both Cypriote and Rhodian finds, e.g. RDAC 1978, 162, 184 pl. 23.36, from Kazaphane near Kyreneia, BMSculpture I 2, 26, C 30 fig. 25, from Tamassos, BMSculpture I, 1, 162-163, B 338-339 fig. 200, both from Kameiros. For the modelling of the face, see SCE III, 585-587 pls. 185, 187.4 and 188.3, from Arsos, styles I-II. A pair of flutes, from Athens, is actually held in the Danish National Museum, Inv.Nos. 14411-14412, Ars Antiqua Auktion III, Lucerne 1961, 57 No. 144 pl. 56, Dansk Aarbog for Musikforskning 1966-1967, 3-9; see also BCH 108 1984, 111 note 2. For the phorbeia, see now BCH 110 1986, 205-218.

16. Beardless head, presumably male

The hair is hanging in a broad mass down the nape. Over the forehead a diadem with vertical incisions between raised bands marking the horizontal edges. White limestone with light yellowish patina. Remains of red colour on the mouth. Fracture below. Some scratches. H. 0.099 m.

Inv.No. 10434. Provenience, Lindos, Akropolis. Acquired 1942 from the Carlsberg Foundation. – Lindos I, 423 No. 1691 pl. 69, SCE IV 2, 328 note 4, G. Kaulen, Daidalika, Munich 1967, 57, 94, 195, K 11.

Closely related to No. 42 and most likely from a figure resembling one from Golgoi published in Atlas of the Cesnola Collection I, pl. 25.60, 61 and 63; cf. SIMA 20.4 1972, 17 no. 17, 51 pl. 17.2, from the Cesnola Collection, BMSculpture I 2, 14, C 4 figs. 4-5, from Idalion, and ClRh 6/7 1932/3, 284 fig. 7, from Kameiros. The rendering of the face is rather old-fashioned, cp. SCE III, 585-588 pls. 187.4 and 189.1, from Arsos, styles I-III. Compare also BMSculpture I 1, 191-192, B 452 fig. 230, from the sanctuary of Apollon at Naukratis, and Samos VII, Bonn 1968, C 162 pl. 106, from the Samian Heraion.

17. Standing woman

The hair is gathered in a large braid hanging down the back. The right hand is held in front of the breast, the left hangs down at the side; both hands are clenched. The woman is clad in a dress, apparently a tunic, covering the arms to the wrists and with a square neck; a kolpos is concealing a girdle. White limestone with light drab patina. Slight traces of red colour on the left shoulder and at the hips, marking the borders of the dress. The nose and the lower part of the figure are missing, the surface somewhat scratched. H. 0.098 m.

Inv.No. 11326. Provenience: Broulia (Vroulia), so-called chapel. Acquired 1942 from the Carlsberg Foundation. – Vroulia 11, 15 No. 1 pls. 13.2 and 14.2, Lindos I, 402.

A corresponding rendering of the arm hanging down: SCE III pl. 187.2, from Arsos, style I. For the kolpos, see SCE IV 2, 350 pl. 188.7, from Arsos, style II. For the face, ibid. 585-588 pls. 187.3-4, 188.1 and 3, 189.1, from Arsos, styles I-III.

18. Lower part of standing figure, presumably female

The right arm is hanging down, and the hand lies flat against the body. The garment is a long dress, probably a wide tunic, with a kolpos and covering the arm to the wrist. The back is flat. White limestone with light yellowish patina. Black colour indicates the horizontal border of the dress as well as the two converging free ends of a girdle concealed by the kolpos. Two parallel red stripes mark the side borders of the dress and seem to indicate that the left hand was held in front of the chest. With the exception of the right instep both feet are missing. Composed of two fragments. H. 0.118 m.

Inv.No. 10432. Provenience: Lindos, Akropolis. Acquired 1942 from the Carlsberg Foundation. – Lindos I, 422 No. 1679 pl. 68.

The clothing is the same as on No. 17. The same dress and girdle are also found on a statuette related to the early Arsos figures, Gazette Archéologique 8 1883, 330-334 pl. 56, cf. SCE III pls. 185-187.3, 188.3, from Arsos, styles I-II.

19. Upper part of female figure, presumably standing

The right hand is placed in front of the chest and holds a two-handled bowl, apparently a kantharos. The hair is hanging in a broad mass down the nape and the back; it is terminated horizontally. In the lobe of the ear a disc-shaped ornament. White limestone with light yellowish patina. Black colour indicates the bulk of the hair, the eyebrows and the eyes; also traces of black on the bowl. Red colour is used for the line of the hair over the forehead, for nostrils and lips, for the centre of the ear ornament. Red colour alone indicates a necklace with an oblong pendant, and on breast and upper arms the borders of the dress, probably a tunic, which is also shown in this manner with a triangular opening at the neck. On the outer side of the bowl, on its upper side, which is not hollowed out, and on the handle there are red dots. The lower part of the left arm is missing. H. 0.075 m.

Inv.No. 10428. Provenience: Lindos, Akropolis. Acquired 1942 from the Carlsberg Foundation. – Lindos I, 415 No. 1632 pl. 66.

A similar figure with a bowl in its left hand was discovered in the sanctuary of Apollon at Naukratis, BMSculpture I 1, 191-192, B 452 fig. 230, others with the bowl in the right hand and with a carved necklace of beads come from Kition, Idalion and Arsos, BMSculpture I 2, 95-96, C 234-236 figs. 155-156, SCE III, 585-587 pls. 187.1 and 188.5, styles I-II. Related faces occurred at Golgoi, AJA 78 1974, 289 pl. 62.5-6, at Kazaphane near Kyreneia, RDAC 1978, 169, 184 pl. 21.80 and at Arsos, SCE III, 586-588 pls. 187.3 and 189.1, styles II-III, cf. also our No. 17.

20. Upper part of female figure

The hair, which is parted in the middle, is hanging in a broad mass down over the shoulders. Flat back. White limestone with light yellowish patina. Most of the arms and a piece of the left shoulder are missing. Composed of three fragments. H. 0.089 m.

Inv.No. 7674. Provenience: probably the island of Rhodes. Acquired 1921 from K.F. Kinch's collection. – Lindos I, 402, NMVAntiksamlingen[4], Copenhagen 1935, 27 No. 56, G. Kaulen, Daidalika, Munich 1967, 96-97 figs. 8-9.

Closely related to our No. 19 and the pieces compared with it. For the face, see also Atlas of the Cesnola Collection I pl. 10.12, from Golgoi, SCE III, 587-588 pl. 189.1, from Arsos, style III.

21. Upper part of seated female figure

The hair is hanging in a thick mass down in front of each shoulder. At the back the upper part of a chair back. White limestone with light yellowish patina. Red colour is used for the lips and to indicate the rectangular neck-border of a dress. Most of the arms and the corners of the chair-back are missing; the surface has some scratches. H. 0.049 m.

Inv.No. 10443. Provenience: Lindos, Akropolis. Acquired 1942 from the Carlsberg Foundation. – Lindos I, 442 No. 1784 pl. 73.

For the figure type, see Nos. 60 ff below. As far as the facial features are concerned, No. 21 is the latest of our Early Archaic human series and leads directly to Nos. 46 and 53-55. Cp. SCE III 587-588 pl. 189.1, from Arsos, style III.

22. Miniature hypokraterion (?)

The lower part is shaped like a truncated cone crowned by a projection resembling a collar of leaves. The upper part is funnel-shaped, not hollow, but with a shallow circular depression (diam. 0.029 m, depth 0.018 m), probably intended to hold a bowl of some kind, and decorated with three beardless relief busts, the hair of which hangs down in a thick mass on each shoulder. Only one of the busts has the eyes indicated. White limestone with light yellowish patina. Composed of several fragments. Edges and adjacent parts in some places missing. H. 0.178 m.

Inv.No. 10467. Provenience: Lindos, Akropolis. Acquired 1942 from the Carlsberg Foundation. – Lindos I, 457-458 No. 1858 pl. 79.

The shape of the object recalls certain Oriental and Orientalizing conical stands, T.M. Cross, Bronze Tripods and Related Stands in the Eastern Mediterranean from the Twelfth through the Seventh Centuries B.C., Ann Arbor 1974, 57-58, 80, 94-95, 99-109, 117-118, 122-125, 152-186, 203-204, 209-225. In spite of the summary carving the faces have so much stylistic character that it is possible to compare them with works like SCE III 587-588 pl. 189.1, from Arsos, style III, and H. Payne & G.M. Young, Archaic Marble Sculpture from the Acropolis, London 1936, 1 note 1 pl. 17.1-2, Schrader, Marmorbildwerke, 330-332 Nos. 451-452 figs. 384-386.

23. Seated lion (Lion séjant)

Open jaws with pendant tongue. The tail coils up along the right hind leg. The lion is seated on a plinth, rectangular in front, but rounded behind and with a convex upper side. White limestone with light yellowish patina. On tongue, lips, nostrils and in the ears faint remains of red colour. Composed of five fragments; minor parts are missing. H. 0.115 m.

Inv.No. 10453. Provenience: Lindos, Akropolis. Acquired 1942 from the Carlsberg Foundation. – Lindos I, 453 No. 1825 pl. 77, Salamine de Chypre IV, 27 pl. 9 a-b, Kypern, fra stenalder til romertid, Ny Carlsberg Glyptotek, Copenhagen 1983, 61 No. 167.

The same type of lion is represented among the finds from Kameiros, Chios, the Knidian peninsula and Naukratis, BMSculpture I 1, 168-169, B 371-380 pl. 38, ClRh 6/7 1932/3, 282, I 11, 285 fig. 9, BSASuppl 6 1967, 181, 185 Nos. 1-2 pl. 68, SCE IV 2, 333 fig. 5 m,

BMSculpture I 1, 200, B 470-471 fig. 243, B 470 from the sanctuary of Apollon; but it is also known from the Salamis region in Cyprus, Salamine de Chypre IV, 19-45 pls. 6-8, and from the South Palestinian coast-land, ᶜAtiqot 6/7 1966/7, 22 No. 118 pl. 16, from Tall at-Ṭūyūr east of Askalon. With the head turned aside the type occurs on a gravestone from Amathous, Atlas of the Cesnola Collection I pl. 95.642, cf. 641, from Golgoi, cf. a head with traces of red colour, ibid. pl. 84.548, also from Golgoi. The Oriental origin of the type and its Greek relatives have been dealt with by H. Payne, Necrocorinthia, Oxford 1931, 67, 173, and J. Nizette-Godfroid, AntCl 41 1972, 5-48. Cp. also the 9th-century lions from Hama, H. Ingholt, Rapport préliminaire sur sept campagnes de fouilles à Hama en Syrie, Copenhagen 1940, 109-113 pls. 36.3, 37.1-3, NMArb 1943, 50 fig. 14, Hama II 3, Copenhagen 1948, 198-199, Hama II 1, Copenhagen 1948, 205, 208, 236, 268, Sūkās I, Copenhagen 1970, 169 fig. 60, 170.

24. Seated lion (Lion séjant)

The limitation of the mane is indicated by means of an incised line. On eyes, tongue and lips and in the ears remains of red colour. H. 0.092 m.

Inv.no. 10455. Provenience: Lindos, Akropolis. Acquired 1942 from the Carlsberg Foundation. – Lindos I, 454 No. 1830 pl. 77, Salamine de Chypre IV, 27 pl. 9 c-d.

25. Seated lion (Lion séjant)

The limitation of the mane is indicated by means of an incised line. On tongue and lips and in the ear remains of red colour; red is also used for the contours of the eyes. The right ear is missing. On the left cheek and shoulder traces of rust. H. 0.083 m.

Inv.No. 10457. Provenience: Lindos, Akropolis. Acquired 1942 from the Carlsberg Foundation. – Lindos I, 454 No. 1834, AntCl 41 1972, 25 note 70 pl. 11.21.

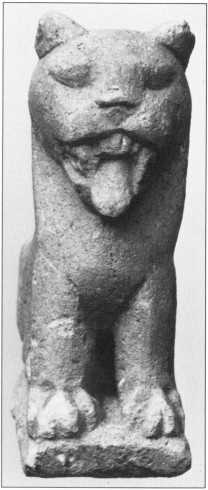

26. Seated Lion (Lion séjant)

On tongue and lips and in the ears faint traces of red colour, and also remains of a red line delimiting the face. The left ear somewhat damaged. H. 0.126 m.

Inv.No. 10458. Provenience: Lindos, Akropolis. Acquired 1942 from the Carlsberg Foundation. – Lindos I, 454 No. 1834.

27. Seated lion (Lion séjant)

The limitation of the mane is indicated by means of an incised line. On tongue, lips, nostrils and ruff of fur traces of red colour. The outline and iris of the right eye are shown in black. The ears, the front legs and the front part of the plinth are missing. H. 0.119 m.

Inv.No. 10456. Provenience: Lindos, Akropolis. Acquired 1942 from the Carlsberg Foundation. – Lindos I, 454 No. 1833 pl. 77.

For the chronology of the type, cp. also Samos VII, 82, C 175 pl. 115, which is rather close to our No. 27 and dates from the time before the Rhoikos constructions, i.e. before c. 560/50 B.C.

28. Seated lion (Lion séjant)

Open jaws with pendant tongue, the longitudinal furrow of which is indicated. The tail coils up along the left hind leg. The lion is seated on a plinth, rectangular in front, rounded behind and with a convex upper side. White limestone with light yellowish patina. On tongue, lips and nostrils and in the ears remains of red colour, also red contours of the eyes, a red line delimiting the face, and red lines on the front paws. The surface damaged in places. H. 0.137 m.

Inv.No. 10454. Provenience: Lindos, Akropolis. Acquired 1942 from the Carlsberg Foundation. – Lindos I, 454 No. 1829 pl. 77, Salamine de Chypre IV, 27 pl. 9 g, Kypern, fra stenalder til romertid, Ny Carlsberg Glyptotek, Copenhagen 1983, 61 No. 168.

For the type, see No. 23 above.

29. Seated lion (Lion séjant)

In the right side of the neck two incised signs are preserved, one representing the syllable *ti* or *ri*, the other a dividing line. The patina is light drab-coloured in places. Some larger pits in the surface of the stone. The upper right part of the head, the front legs and the front part of the plinth are missing. H. 0.154 m.

Inv.No. 7676. Provenience: presumably the island of Rhodes. Acquired 1921 from K.F. Kinch's collection. – Lindos I, 402, NMVAntiksamlingen[4], Copenhagen 1935, 27 No. 56.

For the signs, see O. Masson, Les inscriptions chypriotes syllabiques, Paris 1961, 58 fig. 1, 64 fig. 44, 180 No. 167.

30. Head, neck and chest of lion, presumably seated (séjant)

Open jaws with pendant tongue. The limitation of the mane is indicated by means of an incised line; the ruff of fur is faintly offset from the chest. White limestone with light brownish yellow to greyish patina. Rather damaged on edges and projecting parts. H. 0.129 m.

Inv.No. 10459. Provenience: Lindos, Akropolis. Acquired 1942 from the Carlsberg Foundation. – Lindos I, 454 No. 1834.

This fragment is closely related to Nos. 23-29 above. For the date, cp. also Samos VII, 82, C 175 pl. 115, which is rather similar to No. 30 and of the time before the Rhoikos constructions, i.e. before c. 560/50 B.C.

31. Fragment of lion-fighter group

Of the body of the lion small parts of the front legs and the backwards turned head are preserved, while at the right cheek are the remains of the fighter's arm or leg. White limestone with light yellowish patina. On the lion's muzzle and tongue remains of red colour. The surface in several places worn or knocked off. L. 0.076 m.

Inv.No. 10441. Provenience: Lindos, Akropolis. Acquired 1942 from the Carlsberg Foundation. – Lindos I, 438 No. 1774.

It is only possible to get a very imperfect idea of the representation. However, it is most likely that the fighter was of the Herakles-Melqart type grasping the lion's hind legs and tail so that the front legs were hanging down. In this way the backward turn of the head is more easily understandable, and in that case the preserved remains of the fighter will be part of one of his legs, cf. BMSculpture I 2, 82-84, C 208-209 figs. 133-134 (C 209 found at Idalion), where likewise only the forepart of the lion touches the fighter's leg, and where also the head is turned completely back, not to the side as in BMSculpture I 1, 189-190, B 448 pl. 40, from the sanctuary of Apollon at Naukratis. On the other hand, our No. 31 is earlier than the parallels quoted from Cyprus, as the lion type is the same as that of Nos. 23-30 above; the lion is reasonably well proportioned, like that of the Naukratis group, and not of a reduced size as in later representations. For Herakles-Melqart, see Sūkās VI, Copenhagen 1979, 67-68 and below No. 70.

32. Seated sphinx

The wings are sickle-shaped, upward-curved and not parted. On the head an Egyptian double crown. The hair is hanging in a broad mass down over the shoulders. The chest and the upper parts of the forelegs are covered by a quadrangular "apron". The tail coils up along the right hind leg. The sphinx is seated on a plinth rounded behind and with a convex upper surface. White limestone with light yellowish patina. On the mouth slight traces of red colour. Composed of two fragments. the paws of the forelegs and the front part of the plinth are missing; the surface has been somewhat damaged. H. 0.107 m.

Inv.No. 10450. Provenience: Lindos, Akropolis. Acquired 1942 from the Carlsberg Foundation. – Lindos I, 448 No. 1813 pl. 75.

The shape of the trunk, the legs and the plinth correspond to that of the lions Nos. 23-29 above, the face to that of the female figure No. 19. Very similar sphinxes have been found at Kameiros, BMSculpture I 1, 167-168, B 364-365 pl. 38. For the occurrence of the type in a Phoenicianized milieu, see, for example, the representation on a Cypriote silver bowl from the first half of the 6th century B.C., OpArch 4 1946, 13-14 pl. 14.

33. Seated sphinx

On the conical part of the crown and on the lips remains of red colour. On the "apron" remains of two horizontal red stripes. Composed of four fragments. The point of the crown, the forelegs, the entire hind part and the plinth are missing; minor superficial damage in addition. H. 0.088 m.

Inv.No. 10451. Provenience: Lindos, Akropolis. Acquired 1942 from the Carlsberg Foundation. – Lindos I, 448 No. 1815 pl. 75.

34. Seated sphinx

The wings are sickle-shaped, upwards-curved and not parted. To judge from the fractures the tail coiled backwards and upwards and touched the wings. The sphinx is seated on a rectangular plinth with a convex upper surface. On the outer side of the right wing indistinct remains of an incised Phoenician inscription: . . . t (or š) ṣ m z (or g) . g (or n) ḫ (or ṯ) q k š (reading suggested by Professor B. Otzen, University of Aarhus). White limestone ▷

with light yellowish brown patina. Head, chest, the upper front part of the forelegs and the entire tail are missing; there is in addition minor damage to the surface. H. 0.185 m.

Inv.No. 11328. Provenience: Broulia (Vroulia), so-called chapel. Acquired 1942 from the Carlsberg Foundation. – Vroulia 11, 16 No. 3 pl. 14.4, Lindos I, 402, 446.

Related to our Nos. 32-33; but the coil of the tail rather recalls the figures BMSculpture I 1, 167-168, B 364-365 pl. 38, from Kameiros. The occurrence of a Phoenician inscription on a Cypriot object found in a sanctuary near the south point of the island of Rhodes should not occasion astonishment, as it seems that in the 8th-6th centuries B.C. there was a small settlement of Phoenicians at Ialysos in Rhodes, BICS 16 1969, 1-8, Madrider Beiträge 8 1982, 269, 274.

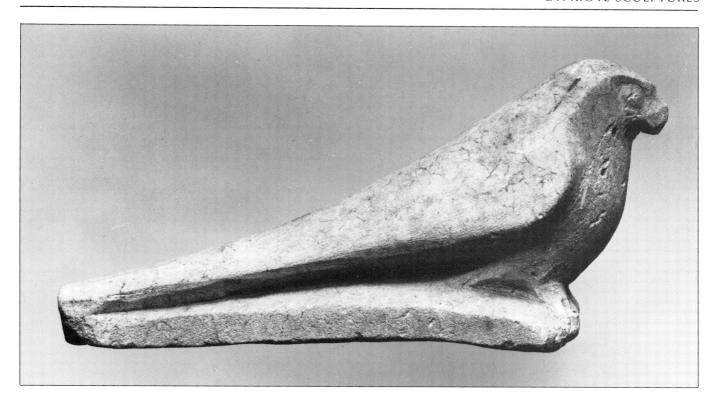

35. Seated bird of prey (falcon?)

Oblong plinth following the outline of the bird. White limestone with light yellowish patina. On the beak and at the nape remains of red paint. The feathers of the tail are indicated by means of series of red Vs, and on both edges of the tail there is a red stripe. Some minor damage of the surface. L. 0.168 m.

Inv.No. 10460. Provenience: Lindos, Akropolis. Acquired 1942 from the Carlsberg Foundation. – Lindos I, 456 No. 1844 pls. 78-79.

Similar figures of birds have been found elsewhere on Rhodes, BMSculpture I 1, 169, B 384 pl. 38, ClRh 6/7 1932/3, 286, I 16 fig. 10, from Kameiros, and our No. 38, from Broulia; but they have also been discovered near Knidos, on Samos, and on Cyprus, Lindos I, 456, SCE IV 2, 128-129, Samos VII, 72, C 83 pl. 112, Salamine de Chypre IV, 30 pl. 10 a-b. In the shaping of the body they recall the Egyptian wooden figures of the Late Period, as well as faience figures manufactured at Naukratis, e.g. A. Erman, Die ägyptische Religion, Berlin & Leipzig 1934, 288 fig. 114, V. Schmidt, Levende og døde i det gamle Ægypten, Copenhagen 1919, 203 figs. 1147-1149, Lindos I, 346 Nos. 1243-1244 pls. 54-55, and our note 66.

36

36

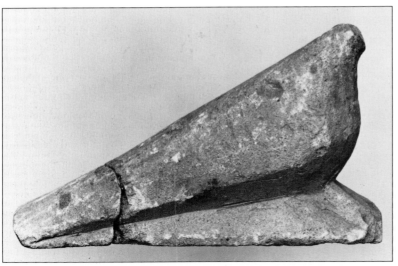

37

37

36. Seated bind of prey (falcon?)

Remains of red colour on cheeks, neck and beak. On the tail some red dots arranged in rows, and on the edges of the tail remains of a red stripe. The point of the beak is missing. The surface damaged in places. L. 0.086 m.

Inv.No. 10461. Provenience: Lindos, Akropolis. Acquired 1942 from the Carlsberg Foundation. – Lindos I, 456 No. 1845.

37. Seated bind of prey (falcon?)

Diminutive head. The patina is brownish yellow in places. Assembled of two fragments. Minor surface damage. L. 0.098 m.

Inv.No. 10465. Provenience: Lindos, Akropolis. Acquired 1942 from the Carlsberg Foundation. – Lindos I, 457 No. 1855.

The figures BMSculpture I 1, 169, B 384 pl. 38, from Kameiros, and Lindos I, 456 No. 1841 pl. 78, from Lindos, have a similar small head.

38

38

39

39

38. Seated bird of prey (falcon?)

Light yellowish brown patina. The tail, the hind-part of the plinth, the left foot, the left front corner of the plinth, and most of the plinth's right edge are missing, in addition to minor surface damage. L. 0.068 m.

Inv.No. 11329. Provenience: Broulia (Vroulia), so-called chapel. Acquired 1942 from the Carlsberg Foundation. – Vroulia 11, 16-17 No. 4 pl. 14.5, Lindos I, 402, 456.

39. Seated bird of prey (falcon?)

As no 38, but with a steeper posture and a shorter tail. The point of the beak is missing. The surface is damaged in places. H. 0.086 m.

Inv.No. 10462. Provenience: Lindos, Akropolis. Acquired 1942 from the Carlsberg Foundation. – Lindos I, 456 No. 1847.

The shaping of the body, the feet and the plinth recurs in the dove figure Atlas of the Cesnola Collection I pl. 80.524, from Golgoi.

40

40

41

41

40. Seated bird of prey (falcon?) holding a small bird in its beak

The legs have been carved in the round. White limestone with light yellowish patina. On both sides of the head a vertical, slightly curved red line, and on the left wing faint remains of red colour. Feet and tail are missing. H. 0.044 m.

Inv.No. 10463. Provenience: Lindos, Akropolis. Acquired 1942 from the Carlsberg Foundation. – Lindos I, 456 No. 1849 pl. 79.

A more complete specimen of the same type: Lindos I, 457 No. 1850 pl. 79; others found in the same Archaic fill, but not illustrated, ibid. 46, 456-457 Nos. 1848 and 1851. The same rendering of the legs recurs, for example, on Lindos I, 456 No. 1846 pl. 79. See also Samos VII, 64-65, C 79 pl. 113.

41. Seated bird of prey (falcon?) holding a snake in its beak

The legs have only in part been carved in the round, the tail of the snake filling the space between the legs and body of the bird. White limestone with light yellowish patina. On the front of the neck remains of red paint. The tail and feet as well as most of the snake's tail are missing. H. 0.061 m.

Inv.No. 10464. Provenience: Lindos, Akropolis. Acquired 1942 from the Carlsberg Foundation. – Lindos I, 457 No. 1853.

An entire figure of the same type comes likewise from Lindos: Lindos I, 457 No. 1852 pl. 79, but the head of the snake hangs down on the opposite side. Cp. also Samos VII, 72, C 80 pl. 112.

MATURE ARCHAIC

C. 565-525 B.C.

No. 42 is without doubt the earliest piece in this series, its face and shoulders being carved in a way corresponding to the modelling of advanced Eastern Greek works[117] while keeping some earlier style elements[118]. The majority of our Mature Archaic fragments with heads preserved (Nos. 45, 46, 52-56, 61 and 68) mark a stage in the development which in Ionian plastic art is represented by the well-known small Samian bronze group of three figures[119]. Contemporary with these is our merman No. 67, who may be compared with Ionian terracottas[120]. The pendulous kolpos of Nos. 43, 48, 61, 62 and 65 recurs on slightly earlier Ionian pieces[121], and a similar way of shaping the seated figure is also found in the same East Greek sphere[122]. The type of sphinx with crossed forelegs recalls a Milesian lion[123], and, of course, its Egyptian ancestors. With its broad chin No. 60 has something in common with an East Greek head[124]. The latest among our Mature Archaic pieces are Nos. 57 and 63, where the "Archaic smile" is beginning to appear, and where also other details connect them with an Ionian bronze[125].

42. Upper part of beardless male figure, presumably standing

The hair is hanging in a broad mass down the nape and the neck. Over the forehead a diadem with vertical incisions between the raised borders. White limestone with light yellowish patina. Red colour is used for the raised borders of the diadem and to indicate the band fastening the diadem around the nape. Nostrils and lips are likewise red, and a red dot on the lobe of the ears may represent a disc-shaped ear-ornament. On the left cheek a red dot. To judge from remains of red colour at the throat the figure was represented as wearing a dress with a rectangular neck-opening. The arms are missing; some superficial damage. H. 0.084 m.

Inv.No. 10425. Provenience: Lindos, Akropolis. Acquired 1942 from the Carlsberg Foundation. – Lindos I, 409 No. 1604 pl. 65, ClRh 6/7 1932/3, 282, G. Kaulen, Daidalika, Munich 1967, 56, 82, 94, 195, K 2.

Similar fragments have been found at Kameiros, near Knidos, on Samos, and on several Cypriote sites, e.g. Idalion and Golgoi, BMSculpture I 1, 166, B 361 pl. 37, ClRh 6/7 1932/33, 284 fig. 7, Lindos I, 409, SCE IV 2, 332-333 fig. 52, Samos VII, 72, C 126 pl. 109, C 159 pl. 99, BMSculpture I 2, 14-15, C 5 fig. 5, Atlas of the Cesnola Collection I pl. 25.60, 61, 63 and 64, pl. 57.385. For the facial features, cp. SCE III, 587-588 pls. 189.1-3 and 190.1, from Arsos, styles III-IV, and from Kazaphane near Kyreneia, RDAC 1978, 168, 184 pl. 22.73.

43. Standing beardless man playing the double flute (auloi)

The hair is hanging in a broad mass down the nape. The man wears a long dress covering the shoulders, apparently a tunic; around the waist a broad belt, at the sides concealed by a pendulous kolpos. A flute-case hangs in a strap over the left shoulder. Flat back. White limestone with light yellowish patina. The legs are missing; the flutes and the hands damaged. H. 0.098 m.

Inv.No. 10436. Provenience: Lindos, Akropolis. Acquired 1942 from the Carlsberg Foundation. – Lindos I, 426 No. 1707 pl. 70, S. Dietz & S. Trolle, Arkæolo-gens Rhodos, Copenhagen 1974, 63 fig. 63 left, Kypern, fra stenalder til romertid, Ny Carlsberg Glyptotek, Copenhagen 1983, 61 No. 163.

Another flute-player with the flute-case on the shoulder: BMSculpture I 2, 26, C 30 fig. 25, from Tamassos. A flute-player with the same modelling of the body and head, but of larger size: Atlas of the Cesnola Collection I pl. 13.15, from Golgoi. A similar belt and kolpos: ibid. pl. 16.21, from Kourion. Our No. 43 is considerably later than the flute-player No. 15 above, and, as far as the facial features are concerned, is rather to be compared with works like SCE III, 587-588 pls. 189.2 and 190.5, from Arsos, style IV.

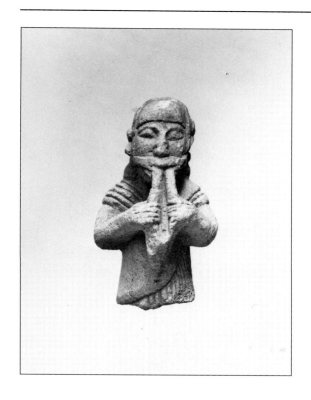

44. Standing beardless man playing the double flute (auloi)

The hair is hanging in a broad mass down the nape. Around the head a mouth-band (phorbeia) with a supporting band over the crown of the head. The man wears a long dress, apparently a tunic, which in front is portrayed with close longitudinal folds, and which leaves the arms bare. Over it a rounded cloak passing under the right arm and over the left shoulder. White limestone with light yellowish patina. The borders of the cloak are indicated in red colour, also on the back of the figure. The entire lower part of the figure including the ends of the flutes is missing. H. 0.055 m.

Inv.No. 10437. Provenience: Lindos, Akropolis. Acquired 1942 from the Carlsberg Foundation. – Lindos I, 426-427 No. 1710 pl. 70, Kypern, fra stenalder til romertid, Ny Carlsberg Glyptotek, Copenhagen 1983, 60-61 No. 162.

Mouth-band rendered in the round, possibly with supporting band over the crown of the head: Atlas of the Cesnola Collection I pl. 21.42, 44 and 48, from Golgoi, RDAC 1978, 163, 184 pl. 23.40, from Kazaphane near Kyreneia. Flute-player wearing a cloak: Atlas of the Cesnola Collection I pl. 21.48, from Golgoi, BMSculpture I 2, 25-26, C 27 fig. 23, from Idalion, SCE III, 56-57 pl. 13.4, from Kition. As far as the facial features are discernible they seem to place the figure chronologically between our Nos. 15 and 43.

45. Standing beardless man (?)

The hair is parted in the middle and is hanging in a broad mass down the nape and the back, in its lower part pointed. The arms hang down with the hands flat to the body. The person wears a long dress, probably a tunic, with a triangular neck-opening; it covers part of the upper arms and has a broad belt, which is not concealed by any kolpos. Apart from the outline of the hair the back is quite flat without any details. White limestone with light yellowish patina. The lower part of the figure is missing, as is also the tip of the nose and a few other parts of the surface. H. 0.112 m.

Inv.No. 10430. Provenience: Lindos, Akropolis. Acquired 1942 from the Carlsberg Foundation. – Lindos I, 419 No. 1663 pl. 68, S. Dietz & S. Trolle, Arkæologens Rhodos, Copenhagen 1974, 63 fig. 63 right.

Related, but later: SCE III, 56-57 pl. 8, from Kition. The face recalls SCE III, 587-588 pls. 189.2, 190.1, 5, 7 and 8, from Arsos, style IV. The faint smile is a presage of the approaching Late Archaic style (Arsos V).

46. Standing beardless man with a he-goat standing at his left side

The man's left hand holds the right horn of the goat, and the animal's forelegs rest on his feet. The man's hair is hanging in a broad mass down the nape. He is clad in a long dress exposing the arms and without a belt, probably a tunic. Irregular ob- long plinth, convex in front, with the upper side shaped like a ridge-roof. White limestone with light yellowish patina. Red colour is used for the lips of the man and to indicate the borders and shoulder-seam of his dress; there is also red on the forehead ▷

and the mouth of the goat. The man's right elbow, the right hand, the left arm with exception of the hand, the tip of the nose and the chin are missing; the surface has moreover some minor scratches. H. 0.176 m.

Inv.No. 10439. Provenience: Lindos, Akropolis. Acquired 1942 from the Carlsberg Foundation. – Lindos I, 428, 434 No. 1750 pl. 71, ClRh 6/7 1932/3, 280, Kypern, fra stenalder til romertid, Ny Carlsberg Glyptotek, Copenhagen 1983, 60 No. 158.

The type recurs at Kameiros, but with the goat at the right side: ClRh 6/7 1932/3, 280, I 1 fig. 1. Related representations have been found at Golgoi: Atlas of the Cesnola Collection I pls. 27.71 and 28.136. The modelling of the face corresponds to styles II and IV at Arsos, SCE III, 587-588 pls. 188.2 and 189.2. The goat as an attribute or sacrificial animal may hint at a cult of Baᶜal Ḥammān, cf. Nos. 64-65 below.

47. Standing man carrying a goat recumbent on his right arm

The left arm is hanging down with the hand clenched. The man wears a long dress which leaves the arms bare, evidently a tunic. Flat back. White limestone with light yellowish patina. Red colour indicates the borders of the dress along its shoulder-seam; there is also red on the forehead and the ear of the goat. On the back an incised inscription: hεκατιος. The man's head, the lower part of his dress, and his feet are missing. H. 0.147 m.

Inv.No. 10440. Provenience: Lindos, Akropolis. Acquired 1942 from the Carlsberg Foundation. – Lindos I, 429, 435-436 No. 1765 fig. 54 pl. 72, Kypern, fra stenalder til romertid, Ny Carlsberg Glyptotek, Copenhagen 1983, 60 No. 159.

Similar figures have been found at Arsos, Golgoi, Kameiros, and on the Knidian peninsula, SCE III, 588 pl. 190.4, style IV, Atlas of the Cesnola Collection I pl. 28.137, BMSculpture I 1, 163-164, B 341, fig. 202, SCE IV 2, 333 fig. 5 c and o. The inscription, probably a dedication, may be explained as an adjective derived from , Ἕκατος "the Smiter", i.e. Apollo, or from, Ἑκάτη "the Smitress", i.e. Artemis or Hekate, cf. W. Pape, Wörterbuch der griechische Eigennamm[3] I, Braunschweig 1870, 339: Ἑκατήϊος, "belonging to Hekate".

48. Standing man carrying a ram on his shoulders

The left hand holds the animal's hind legs, the right one its forelegs. The man wears a long dress, probably a tunic, which leaves the arms bare; at the waist a broad belt, concealed at the sides by a pendulous kolpos. The back is flat and without details except an incised line limiting the belly of the animal. White limestone with light brownish yellow patina. The dress borders and the belt are painted red. Head and trunk of the animal, the head of the man, and the lower part of the figure are missing. H. 0.080 m.

Inv.No. 10438. Provenience: Lindos, Akropolis. Acquired 1942 from the Carlsberg Foundation. – Lindos I, 430-431 No. 1727 pl. 71.

Figures which are nearly duplicates of No. 48 have been found at Kameiros, on Samos, and at Kourion, ClRh 6/7 1932/3, 280-281, I 2 fig. 2, Samos VII, 72, C 121 pl. 97, Atlas of the Cesnola Collection I pl. 16.21; cf. also ibid. pl. 16.22, from Golgoi, and Perrot & Chipiez III, 433 fig. 307, from Syria.

49. Standing man

The right hand is held before the chest; the left arm is hanging down at the side. Both hands are clenched. The man wears a long dress, evidently a tunic, which leaves the arms bare, and over it there is a rounded cloak covering the right side and arm with exception of the hand, and with the ends passing over the left shoulder. The back is summarily carved without any details. White limestone with light yellowish patina. Along the hems of the dress there are broad red stripes and along those of the cloak a red border consisting of short transverse strokes and a broad stripe. Head, feet and nearly the entire plinth are missing. The surface damaged in places. H. 0.158 m.

Inv.No. 10423. Provenience: Lindos, Akropolis. Acquired 1942 from the Carlsberg Foundation. – Lindos I, 406 No. 1586 pl. 65, C. Blinkenberg, Knidia, Copenhagen 1933, 218.

Such cloak-clad figures are anything but rare in the Cypriote sculpture, see, for example, BMSculpture I 2, 30-32, C 41-46 and 48 figs. 34, 35 and 39, 35-36, C 68 fig. 43, from Tamassos and Idalion, SCE III 55-56 pl. 13.2, from Kition, style I, Atlas of the Cesnola Collection I pl. 42.267-270 and 275-276, pls. 44.281, 47.284 and 55.351-356, from Golgoi, RDAC 1978, 166, 184 pl. 20.55, from Kazaphane near Kyreneia, Renan, Mission de Phénicie 56 pl. 21.3, from Tartūs, Lindos I 406, SCE IV 2, 332-333 fig. 52, from the Knidian peninsula, and Samos VII, 55, C 131 pl. 95, from Samos. The painted border of the cloak is probably to be understood as a trimming of fringes, cf. Lindos I, 406 ad No. 1585, JHS 12 1891, 147 pl. 9, SCE II, 705, 780 pl. 208, Blinkenberg, Knidia, loc.cit.

50. As No. 49

Over the dress a broad belt. Flat back. On the belt a red stripe, along the hem of the cloak a red border consisting of short transverse strokes and a broad stripe. Head, chest, left shoulder and arm with exception of the hand, and the lower part of the figure are missing. H. 0.078 m.

Inv.No. 10424. Provenience: Lindos, Akropolis. Acquired 1942 from the Carlsberg Foundation. – Lindos I, 407 No. 1590.

51. Upper part of male torso

To judge from the fractures the right hand was probably placed before the chest holding some object. The hair is hanging down with long vertical locks in front of the shoulders and on the back. White limestone with yellowish patina. Head and arms are missing. Broken off below. H. 0.046 m.

Inv.No. 10426. Provenience: Lindos, Akropolis. Acquired 1942 from the Carlsberg Foundation. – Lindos I, 410 No. 1610 pl. 65.

The same summary rendering of beaded locks is found on a figure with similar proportions, Atlas of the Cesnola Collection I pl. 20.38, from Golgoi. The right arm may perhaps be reconstructed as on the figure Lindos I, 417 No. 1651 pl. 67. Cf. also BMSculpture I 1, 186, B 442 pl. 40, from the sanctuary of Apollon at Naukratis.

52. Standing winged female deity

The hair is parted in the middle and is hanging in a thick mass down over each shoulder. Around the neck a string of beads with an oblong pendant. The deity wears a long dress which covers the arms to the wrists, perhaps a wide tunic. From the lower part of the trunk spring two pairs of wings, the upper pair covering the abdomen and curving upwards behind the arms and shoulders, whereas the straight lower wings are directed obliquely downward and outward. The hands are placed in front of the abdomen; each of them holds a snake winding along the legs and the body. The figure is standing on a plinth with convex front and sloping upper side. Flat back. White limestone with brownish patina. Remains of red colour indicate the dress's rectangular neck-opening; red is also preserved on the left "sleeve hem". Composed of three fragments. The nose, the points of the upper pair of wings, the heads of the snakes and a short piece at the middle of the right snake are missing. The surface damaged in places. H. 0.225 m.

Inv.No. 7673. Provenience: Kalathos in the island of Rhodes. Acquired 1921 from K.F. Kinch's collection. – Lindos I, 402, NMVAntiksamlingen[4], Copenhagen 1935, 27 No. 56, NMVAntiksamlingen[5], Copenhagen 1948, 41 No. 11 E, Guides to the National Museum, Department of Oriental and Classical Antiquities, Copenhagen 1950, 42 No. 11 E, NMArb 1952, 88 fig. 11, NMVÆgypten og Vestasien, Copenhagen 1968, 64 Nos. 18-19 E, Guide to the National Museum, Egypt and Western Asia, Copenhagen 1968, 69 Nos. 18-19 E.

With three pairs of wings and snakes in her hands a similar female deity is represented on a 9th century orthostat relief from Tall Ḥalāf, the ancient Guzana: Tall Halaf III, Berlin 1955, 92, A 3, 166 pl. 95 a. A frontal naked four-winged fertility goddess with grapes in her hands is portrayed on a North-Syrian or East-Anatolian electrum plaque of the 9th or 8th century B.C., AnSt 30 1980, 169-178 pl. 8, and similar figures holding animals also occur in Syrian and Cypriote art, ibid. 173 pls. 10-11. Wings, on the other hand, are not among the attributes of the Minoan "snake goddess". A male wingless type with snakes known from Cypriote sculptures found at Amathous and on Samos can hardly have anything to do with our No. 52: Atlas of the Cesnola Collection I pl. 32.209, AM 66 1941, 5, 6 note 4, 8 pl. 11; it has been suggested that it may represent a "snake charmer", cf. BMSculpture I 1, 161, B 334 pl. 37, J.L. Myres, Handbook of the Cesnola Collection, New York 1914, 148-149, but there are some Near-Eastern figures of this kind which certainly have a divine character, Sūkās VI, Copenhagen 1979, 40 note 80. As to the modelling of the face, our No. 52 belongs to a stage of stylistic development delimited by specimens like SCE III, 586, 588 pls. 185 and 189.2, from Arsos, styles I and IV. ▷

53. Upper part of female figure, probably standing

To judge from the fractures the right hand was presumably held in front of the body. The hair falls in a broad mass down the nape and the back and is terminated below by a broad horizontal band. In the ears are indistinct ornaments and around the neck a string of beads with an oblong pendant. The woman wears the usual, probably long dress. White limestone with light yellowish patina. Black colour is used for eyes, eyebrows and hair, the broad horizontal band on the back has vertical red strokes, and there is also red colour on the lips, while a broad red stripe on shoulders and breast indicates a rectangular neck-opening in the dress. Most of both arms, from above the elbows, is missing. H. 0.064 m.

Inv.No. 10431. Provenience: Lindos, Akropolis. Acquired 1942 from the Carlsberg Foundation. – Lindos I, 421 No. 1675 pl. 68.

The type is well-known from finds in Cyprus, e.g. BMSculpture I 2, 95-96, C 234-239 figs. 155-157, from Kition and Idalion, Atlas of the Cesnola Collection I pl. 10.12, from Golgoi, SCE III 586-587 pl. 187.1, from Arsos. For the modelling of the face, see the remarks on our No. 52 and AJA 78 1974, 289 pl. 62.5-6, from Golgoi.

54. Standing female figure

The right hand is held in front of the body and holds a flower. The hair is hanging in a broad mass down the nape. There are ornaments on the edges of the ears, and around the neck a string of beads with an oblong pendant. The woman seems to be wearing a long dress covering the arms to the wrists, perhaps a wide tunic. The back has no details. White limestone with light yellowish patina. Red colour is used for the lips, the ear-ornaments and the pendant. A broad red stripe indicates the rectangular neck-opening of the dress. Around the right wrist and on both sides of the side-seam below it is a broad red stripe. The left hand and the entire lower part of the figure are missing; nose, chin and left breast are damaged. H. 0.132 m.

Inv.No. 10427. Provenience: Lindos, Akropolis. Acquired 1942 from the Carlsberg Foundation. – Lindos I, 413 No. 1620 pl. 66, S. Dietz & S. Trolle, Arkæologens Rhodos, Copenhagen 1974, 63 fig. 63, centre.

Similar figures have been found at Kameiros, in the sanctuary of Apollon at Naukratis, and in Cyprus, BMSculpture I 1, 166, B 360 pl. 37, 194-195, B 457 fig. 234, BMSculpture I 2, 96, C 237-238 fig. 157 and SIMA 20.9, 33 No. 109, 90, from Idalion, Atlas of the Cesnola Collection I pl. 10.12, from Golgoi. The type of face recurs in Arsos, style IV, SCE III 588 pls. 189.2-3 and 190.1, 4, 5, 7 and 8. For the ear ornaments, see SCE III 588 pl. 189.2-3, Lindos I, 491 note 1, and our No. 56 below.

55. Upper part of female figure, probably standing

A fracture on the chest seems to indicate that the right hand was positioned in front of it. The hair is hanging in a broad mass down the nape. Over the forehead a diadem, summarily rendered, with faint traces of a row of vertical lines. The woman wears the usual, probably long dress. Flat back. White, somewhat coarse limestone with light yellowish patina. Red colour is used for the lips and the nostrils. Remains of red colour indicate ornaments on the lobe of the ear and around the neck. Faint traces of red on both sides of the neck seem to mark a rectangular neck-opening in the dress. The right arm, most of the left arm, the shoulders and the lower part of the figure are missing; the surface has some scratches. H. 0.095 m.

Inv.No. 7675. Provenience: probably the island of Rhodes. Acquired 1921 from K.F. Kinch's collection. – Lindos I, 402, NMVAntiksamlingen[4], Copenhagen 1935, 27 No. 56.

For the diadem, see Lindos I, 417 No. 1653 pl. 67, BMSculpture I 1, 167, B 362 fig. 206, from Kameiros, ibid. 194-195, B 457 fig. 234, from the sanctuary of Aphrodite at Naukratis, BMSculpture I 2, 98-99, C 253-258 fig. 163, from Achna, Idalion and Kition, SCE III 55-56 pl. 6.4-5, from Kition, style I B, SCE III 588 pl. 190.4, from Arsos, style IV. Several of these figures also have the same dress, ornaments and attitude. The facial features correspond to styles II and IV at Arsos, SCE III 586-588 pls. 188.2, 190.5.

56. Left half of female head

The hair is hanging in a broad mass down the nape. There are ear-ornaments both on the lobe and at the upper edge of the ear. White limestone with light yellowish patina. Broken off below. H. 0.051 m.

Inv.No. 10435. Provenience: Lindos, Akropolis. Acquired 1942 from the Carlsberg Foundation. – Lindos I, 424 No. 1693 pl. 69.

For the ear-ornaments, see our No. 54. For the style, see SCE III 588 pl. 189.2-3, from Arsos, style IV.

57. Beardless head, presumably male

The hair is falling in a broad, horizontally waved mass down the nape; on the crown of the head it is combed forward. Around the hair a plain stephane. The beginning of the shoulders is preserved. Flat back. White limestone with yellowish brown patina. The nose is missing; the surface is damaged in places. Broken off below. H. 0.108 m.

Inv.No. 1511. Provenience: erroneously given as "Palmyra", probably from the Lebanese Tripolis (Ṭarābulus) or its environs. Acquired 1880 from Julius Løytved, Beirut, together with a Roman votive altar from Tripolis, inv.No. 1516. – NMFührer[3], Copenhagen 1908, 67 no. 1, NMVAntiksamlingen[3], Copenhagen 1918, 72 no. 1, MélBeyr 46 1970/1, 227-228 fig. 3.

Related as regards hair style, facial features, or both: BMSculpture I 2, 48-49, C 102-103 figs. 66-67, 100, C 260 fig. 165, from Kition and Idalion, SCE III 56-57 pl. 10.1-2 and 4, from Kition, style II A, cf. also Samos VII, 55, C 163 pl. 96, from the Samian Heraion, according to the circumstances of discovery dating to c. 560, cf. ibid. 98, and BMusBeyr 8 1946-48, 85 No. 82 pl. 38, from ᶜAmrīt.

58. Upper part of female(?) figure (hydrophoros?), presumably standing, carrying a pot on the left shoulder

The pot seems to be a water jug with egg-shaped body and disc-shaped foot; it is supported by the figure's left hand, which grasps the handle. The hair is hanging in a broad mass down the nape. Crude workmanship. White limestone with light yellowish patina. The surface is damaged in many places, particularly on the front. H. 0.081 m.

Inv.No. 10429. Provenience: Lindos, Akropolis. Acquired 1942 from the Carlsberg Foundation. – Lindos I, 418-419 No. 1658 pl. 68.

In spite of the awkward modelling it is possible to assign the fragment to our Mature Archaic series, if we consider the proportions of the face. A hydrophoros which has another object on her left shoulder comes from Idalion: BMSculpture I 2, 99-100, C 259 fig. 164.

59. Lower part of standing person clad in a long dress

The left arm is hanging down with the hand clenched. The figure is standing on a plinth rounded in front and with a sloping upper side. Flat back. Both on the front and on the back incised inscriptions, on the front ƷＩⱢＥＰＨ⊳... (twice), on the back ＮＩＫ⊳ƷＰ∑ＦＩ... White limestone with light yellowish patina. A red stripe marks the horizontal hem of the dress. H. 0.090 m.

Inv.No. 10433. Provenience: Lindos, Akropolis. Acquired 1942 from the Carlsberg Foundation. – Lindos I, 422-423 No. 1688 fig. 52 pl. 68, Kypern, fra stenalder til romertid, Ny Carlsberg Glyptotek, Copenhagen 1983, 61 No. 166.

The garment is the long unbelted dress which we also know from other figures in this series, e.g. Nos. 46-47. For the shape of the plinth, cp. No. 52. The inscription on the front probably reads: Σιτέα ἠμ(ι) (Doric = Attic Σιτείου (εἰμι)), i.e. "I belong to Siteas". The inscription on the back may perhaps be interpreted νικάσας (Doric = Attic νικήσας) πυ (ξξ) (Rhodian = Attic πύξ) or Πύ (θια), i.e. "he who won the boxing contest" or "he who won in the Pythian Games", cf. Lindos II 1, 281-284 No. 68, and II 2, 997-998 No. 701.

60. Beardless head, probably from a figure of a seated woman

The hair hangs down on the shoulders and conceals the ears. Over the forehead a diadem summarily rendered. Behind the body remains of a tall chair-back. White limestone with light greyish patina. On the left side of the diadem very faint remains of vertical red strokes. Also remains of red colour on the lips and on the right shoulder, perhaps indicating the border of the dress. On the hair over the left shoulder traces of rust. Forehead, nose, lips and chin somewhat damaged. H. 0.042 m.

Inv.No. 2126. Provenience: the environs of Ioppe (Yāfā). Acquired 1883 from Valdemar Lausen, M.D. – Den kgl. Antiksamling, Haandkatalog[4], Copenhagen 1884, 18 No. 35, NMFührer[3], Copenhagen 1908, 68 no. 5, NMVAntiksamlingen[3], Copenhagen 1918, 72 no. 5.

With regard to the diadem the fragment should be compared with No. 55 above; but the chair-back indicates a seated figure like Nos. 61 ff. Related facial features occur in Arsos, style IV: SCE III pl. 190.7.

61. Enthroned beardless man

The hands are in the lap holding a small casket with a "button" on the upper surface at the side leaning against the body. The hair hangs in a broad mass down the nape. The person wears a long dress with a kolpos hanging far down at the sides. The arms seem to be bare. The throne has a vertical, rectangular back with the corners elongated upwards and vertical, protruding side-pieces acting as armrests. White limestone with light yellowish patina. The nose and the feet of the figure are missing, as are the corners of the throne-back, part of the left throne-arm and the lower right corner. The surface somewhat scratched and weathered. H. 0.108 m.

Inv.No. 10446. Provenience: Lindos, Akropolis. Acquired 1942 from the Carlsberg Foundation. – Lindos I, 440, 442-443 No. 1791 pl. 74.

A related figure was found in the sanctuary of Apollon at Naukratis, Naucratis I, London 1886, 13 pl. 2.20, BMSculpture I 1, 200, B 468. Cp. the much later figure BMSculpture I 2, 136-137, C 426 fig. 216, from Idalion, and SCE II, 348 pls. 66.41 and 161.4, from Marion. There also seems to be some connection with faience figures like Lindos I, 350-351 No. 1256 pl. 55. The modelling of the face corresponds to that common in Arsos, style IV, SCE III 588 pl. 189.2. The casket may be a container for incense or for the keys of a temple, cf. M. Dunand & R. Duru, Oumm el-ᶜAmed, Paris 1962, 165 note 2.

62. Enthroned beardless man

The hands rest upon the throne-arms. The hair hangs in a broad mass on both shoulders. The person wears a long dress with a belt, which at the sides is concealed by a pendulous kolpos. The throne is of the same type as that of No. 61. Under the feet a foot-stool, protruding a little. White limestone with light brownish patina. The seams of the dress are indicated by a single red stripe on the upper arms and a double one on the shoulders; there is also a red stripe along the neckline and along the lower hem of the dress. The upward elongated corners of the throne-back are missing, while several projecting parts, i.a. the face, are much damaged by blows and scratches. H. 0.095 m.

Inv.No. 10445. Provenience: Lindos, Akropolis. Acquired 1942 from the Carlsberg Foundation. – Lindos I, 442 No. 1787 pl. 74.

A similar figure was found at Kameiros, BMSculpture I 1, 167, B 363 fig. 207; cf. also a 5th century figure from Marion, SCE II, 348 pl. 66.42. Compared with the Arsos sculptures, even if the damaged face is left out of consideration, our No. 62 cannot be later than style IV, SCE III 588 pls. 189-190.

63. Enthroned beardless man

The hands are resting on the seat. The hair is hanging in a thick mass down in front of each shoulder. The person wears a long dress, which apparently does not cover the arms, and over it a cloak passing under the right arm and over the left shoulder. The throne has a box-shaped seat and a rounded vertical back. White limestone with light yellowish patina. Red colour is used for the lips and for the edge of the front hair, while there are also remains of red on the cloak and on the front of the throne. Of the rounded, upward elongated corners of the throne the left one is missing, as well as the right hand and both feet of the figure; there are, in addition, minor marks of blows and scratches. H. 0.071 m.

Inv.No. 10444. Provenience: Lindos, Akropolis. Acquired 1942 from the Carlsberg Foundation. – Lindos I, 442 No. 1786 pl. 74.

Related both to our No. 62 and a figure from the sanctuary of Aphrodite at Naukratis, BMSculpture I 1, 196, B 462 fig. 237, the latter, however, having a different position of the arms. The smiling face indicates that No. 63 belongs to the later part of the Mature Archaic period, cf. SCE III 586-589 pls. 187.4, 188.3 and 208, from Arsos, styles II and V.

64. Enthroned ram-headed deity

The hands are in the lap holding a small casket with a "button" on the upper surface at the side leaning against the body. A broad lock of hair is hanging down in front of each shoulder. The deity wears a long dress, which leaves the arms bare. The throne is of the same type as that of No. 61, but with corners extending slightly upwards. Under the feet a foot-stool, protruding only a little. On the sides of the throne irregularly incised lines probably intended to be parallel. White limestone with light yellowish patina. On the hems of the dress remains of red colour. The muzzle, the upward extending corners of the throne-back, most of the feet and of the footstool, as well as minor fragments are missing; there are also some scratches. H. 0.107 m.

Inv.No. 10447. Provenience: Lindos, Akropolis. Acquired 1942 from the Carlsberg Foundation. – Lindos I, 441, 443 No. 1793 pl. 74. BMSculpture I 1, 159, RStFen 10 1982, 195 note 33.

This type seems a fusion of types like those of No. 61 and 65. Probably the ram-headed figures represent Ammon or the Phoenician Ba°al Ḥammān. For the latter deity, generally taken to be "the Lord of the Incense Altar", see Mélanges René Dussaud 2, Paris 1939, 795-802, and for ram cults in Cyprus, RDAC 1974, 151-155. According to P. Bordreuil (personal communication) Ba°al Ḥammān may originally have been the god of Mount Amanus on the Levant coast facing eastern Cyprus. In any case our figures are related to the Egyptian representations of the ram god, Lindos I, 441, ML I 1, 291, A. Erman, Religion der Ägypter, Berlin & Leipzig 1934, 43-44 fig. 33, but they also resemble certain terracottas from Meniko and Kythraia in Cyprus, from Makmīš in Palestine and °Amrīt in Syria, V. Karageorghis, Two Cypriote Sanctuaries of the End of the Cypro-Archaic Period, Rome 1977, 35-36 No. 1, 45, A. Caubet, La religion à Chypre dans l'antiquité, Lyons 1979, 27 fig. 52, RStFen 10 1982, 189-195 pls. 46-48.1. The dedication of a possibly Phoenician god in Lindos should be viewed in connection with the existence of a Phoenician community on the island, see ad No. 34.

65. Enthroned ram-headed deity

The hands are resting on the throne-arms. A broad lock of hair is hanging down in front of each shoulder. The deity wears a long dress, which seems to leave the arms bare, with a belt which at the sides is concealed by a pendulous kolpos. The throne is of the same type as that of No. 64. Under the feet a protruding foot-stool. White limestone with light yellowish patina. Insignificant damage. H. 0.066 m.

Inv.No. 10448. Provenience: Lindos, Akropolis. Acquired 1942 from the Carlsberg Foundation. – Lindos I, 441, 443 No. 1795 pl. 74, BMSculpture I 1, 159, RStFen 10 1982, 195 note 33.

Same type: BMSculpture I 1, 170, B 390, 167 fig. 207, from Lardos near Lindos, BMSculpture I 2, 89-90, C 222 fig. 144, from Idalion, Atlas of the Cesnola Collection I pls. 38.248 and 250 and 57.373, from Golgoi, SCE III 265-266 pl. 61.4, from Bounoi (Vouni), style II. Our No. 65, however, is probably earlier than the parallels last mentioned, and contemporary with No. 62. For the deity, see ad No. 64.

66. Enthroned woman

The hands are resting on the throne-arms. The hair hangs down in front of both shoulders. The woman wears a long belted dress. The throne seems to have been of the same type as that of No. 63. Under the feet a foot-stool. On the rear side of the throne there is a projecting rectangular panel above, and below it incised lines || ⌐', perhaps the letters ||Y indicating the numbers 10 + 10 + 14 = 34. White limestone with light drab-coloured patina. Head and neck, part of right upper arm, right hand, left elbow, left lower arm and hand, the knees, the edges of the throne-back, the left throne-arm, the front edge of the throne and the lower right corner of its back are missing, in addition to minor damage. H. 0.092 m.

Inv.No. 10442. Provenience: Lindos, Akropolis. Acquired 1942 from the Carlsberg Foundation. – Lindos I, 442 No. 1782.

A related figure was found at Kameiros: BMSculpture I 1, 167, B 363 fig. 207, another, but of much later date in grave 58 at Marion: SCE II 348 pl. 66.42. A similar, no doubt Cypriote figure probably belonged to a burial of c. 550-500 B.C. in the Harbour Necropolis at Sūkās on the North-Phoenician coast, Sūkās VI, Copenhagen 1979, 14-15 No. 16 fig. 24.

67. Merman with human bearded head, trunk and arms, and a fish-tail

In front the hair has twisted locks hanging down over the forehead; behind, the hair hangs down in a broad zigzag-grooved mass over nape and back. The beard only covers the cheeks and chin; it has vertical locks, some of them twisted. The trunk is clad in a dress which leaves the arms bare. The left arm holds a lyre, the right hand a plektron. On the left wrist is a broad band or amulet. The fish-tail has one dorsal fin and two lateral ones. Under the belly a small plinth. White limestone with light yellowish patina. Black colour is used for the hair and the beard, but the forehead is outlined with a ▷

red stripe. Red is also found on the lips. The dress is red except for the edges of the arm-opening and the shoulder-seam. The sound-board of the lyre is also red, and red dots indicate the scales of the fishtail. The tip of the nose, the point of the beard, the upper corners of the lyre, the edges of the plinth and the end of the fish-tail are missing; otherwise there is insignificant damage. H. 0.165 m.

Inv.No. 10452. Provenience: Lindos, Akropolis. Acquired 1942 from the Carlsberg Foundation. – Lindos I, 450-451 No. 1820 pl. 76, AM 57 1932, 134 note 2, Kypern, fra stenalder til romertid, Ny Carlsberg Glyptotek, Copenhagen 1983, 60 No. 161.

More merman figures than this have been found at Lindos: Lindos I, 451-452 Nos. 1821-1824; but otherwise a syrinx-playing male "siren" from Cyprus is the best stylistic parallel to our No. 67: Perrot & Chipiez III, 599-600 fig. 410, M. Collignon, Les statues funéraires dans l'art grec, Paris 1911, 13 fig. 2, A. Caubet, op.cit. 30-31 fig. 59. Lyre-playing was also a subject represented at Golgoi and in Arsos, style II: Atlas of the Cesnola Collection I, 12, 14, SCE III, 586 pl. 188.7. The upper part of the face permits a dating to the same time as our Nos. 52-54. For representations of mermen, see Lindos I, 450 and K. Sheperd, The Fish-Tailed Monster in Greek and Etruscan Art, New York 1940, especially 4-6, 8-9, 16-23. A bearded merman with snakes in his hands figures on a 9th century relief from Tall Halāf (Guzana) and as a type has its roots in Middle Assyrian art, Tall Halaf III pl. 94 a, H. Genge, Nordsyrisch-südanatolische Reliefs, Copenhagen 1979, 133 fig. 95. As a heraldic emblem a similar creature holding dolphins occurs on the coins of the North-Phoenician insular town of Arados from the end of the 5th century B.C. onwards, SNGDanish National Museum 37 1961 pl. 1.1-5, cf. BMCoins, Phoenicia pls. 1.1-7, 2.30-31 and 45.1. A related figure, often without any attribute, recurs on Phoenician seals of the 5th-3rd centuries B.C., E.

Acquaro, S. Moscati & M.L. Uberti, Anecdota Tharsica, Rome 1975, 58 note 52, 67, B 23 pl. 26, D. Harden, The Phoenicians[3], Harmondsworth 1980, 209, 295 pl. 109 h. To judge from the coins, the principal deity in Arados was a male sea-god, identified on issues from the 2nd century B.C. with Poseidon, SNG loc.cit. pl. 2.61-67. The ancient Phoenician name for this deity was Yam, a word which was correctly translated by Philon of Byblos, the Roman historian of Phoenician religion, as Pontos = "sea", G. Contenau, La civilisation phénicienne[2], Paris 1949, 86. Some god-lists from the Late Bronze Age archives of Rãs Šamra-Ugarit also enumerate Yam among the local deities and name immediately thereafter two divine symbols: the spoon-shaped censer and the lyre, Ugaritica V, Paris 1968, 42-64 No. 18 A-B, 45 lines 29-31. So here the lyre is already somehow associated with the sea-god, just as in Roman times the same instrument could be used by Triton, ML V 1157, F. Matz & F. v. Duhn, Antike Bildwerke in Rom II, Leipzig 1881, 369 No. 3165, 372 No. 3170.

68. Lying (couchant) sphinx

The sickle-shaped wings are turned backwards and parted by means of a groove. The head is turned to the right. A broad lock of hair hangs down in front of each shoulder, most distinctly on the left. The paw of the right foreleg is resting on that of the left. Oblong plinth, in front rectangular, and rounded behind. The entire left side of the sphinx is flat and thus characterized as the back of the figure. White limestone with light yellowish patina. Red dots on wing, chest and belly indicate feathers, tufts of hair or teats, also remains of red on the mouth. Insignificant damage. L. 0.096 m.

Inv.No. 10449. Provenience: Lindos, Akropolis. Acquired 1942 from the Carlsberg Foundation. – Lindos I, 447 No. 1805 pl. 75.

Lying sphinxes with crossed front-paws and the head turned towards the spectator: Atlas of the Cesnola Collection I pls. 17.24 and 104.680, from Golgoi, cf. also the couchant lions ibid. pl. 95.635-637, from Salamis and Golgoi, and funerary stelai with lions, also from Golgoi, RDAC 1977, 170-172 pls. 50-52. Although the head is crudely and summarily carved, the style of No. 68 is to be defined as the same as that of, for example, our No. 46. A fragment of a similar figure was found in the Harbour Sanctuary at Sūkās on the North-Phoenician coast and is probably a local work inspired from Cyprus, Sūkās VI, 40-41, 45 fig. 126.

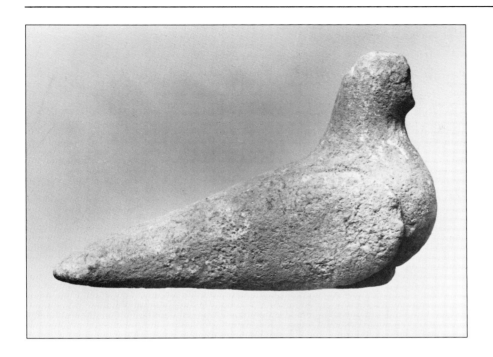

69. Seated bird (dove?)

The legs are indicated in relief on the underside, which has no plinth. White limestone with light yellowish patina. On the legs remains of red colour. The beak and the left side of the head and a piece of the tail are missing; otherwise superficial scratches. L. 0.109 m.

Inv.No. 10466. Provenience: Lindos, Akropolis. Acquired 1942 from the Carlsberg Foundation. – Lindos I, 457 No. 1856 pl. 79.
   Similar, but with a plinth: Atlas of the Cesnola Collection I pl. 80.524 and 526, from Golgoi.

The earliest specimen in this series, No. 71, recalls East Greek works[126], some of which[127] may also be compared with our Nos. 70 and 72; but the latter are a little more stylistically advanced than No. 71. Later still and probably influenced by Attic art are Nos. 73-74[128].

70. Head of beardless Herakles

The crown of the head and the nape are covered with the head part of the lion's skin. The visible front hair is stylized as two horizontal ranges of waves. Above, on the back of the head, there remains a fragment of the club. White limestone with light brown patina. Broken off below. The right ear of the lion's skin is partly missing; some minor damage on the face. H. 0.197 m.

Inv.No. 5037. Provenience: ᶜAmrīt (Marathos). Acquired 1901 from Julius Løytved, Beirut; formerly in the Peretié Collection in Beirut. – NMFührer[3], Copenhagen 1908, 67-68 No. 2, NMVAntiksamlingen[3], Copenhagen 1918, 72 No. 2, NMVAntiksamlingen[4], Copenhagen 1935, 24-25 No. 50, NMVAntiksamlingen[5], Copenhagen 1948, 41 No. 11 F, Guides to the National Museum, Department of Oriental and Classical Antiquities, Copenhagen 1950, 42 No. 11 F, NMArb 1952, 85-86 fig. 7, NMArb 1961, 135, 139 fig. 19 left, AASyr 11/12 1961/2, 143 fig. 19 left, NMVÆgypten og Vestasien, Copenhagen 1968, 64 Nos. 18-19 F, Guides to the National Museum, Egypt and Western Asia, Copenhagen 1968, 69 Nos. 18-19 F, M.-L. Buhl, A Hundred Masterpieces from the Ancient Near East in the National Museum of Denmark, Copenhagen 1974, 72-74 No. 62, Sūkās VI, Copenhagen 1979, 45-46 fig. 139 left, Kypern, fra stenalder til romertid, Ny Carlsberg Glyptotek, Copenhagen 1983, 61 No. 165.

It seems that No. 70 was part of the large find mentioned by Renan, Mission de Phénicie, 850-851; cf. the later finds in the neighbourhood BMusBeyr 7 1944/5, 104 No. 21 pl. 20, BMusBeyr 8 1946-48, 84 No. 21 pl. 34. The type is well-known in Cypriote plastic art: BMSculpture I 2, 84-88, C 213-218 figs. 138-140; it appears c. 540 B.C. and becomes particularly frequent after c. 525 B.C., see SCE III 58-60 pls. 16.3, 22.1-2, 23.1-3, 34.1-3 and 5, 36.1-5, Atlas of the Cesnola Collection I pl. 87.572, 574-576, SIMA 20.5 1974, 32-33 No. 74, 65 fig. 74 a-b, SCE IV 2, 93, 112, 322-323. A fragment of a similar, presumably North-Phoenician, figure in a somewhat later style, of the first half of the 5th century B.C., was found in the Harbour Sanctuary at Sūkās, Sūkās VI, 45-46 No. 21 figs. 137-139. As to the modelling of the face, our No. 70 is obviously earlier than the Herakles figure SCE III 58 pl. 22, from Kition, style III B, and contemporary with works like SCE III 57-59 pls. 17.3 and 19.5, from Kition, style III A. Compare also the somewhat later examples from the Levantine coastland: Syria 56 1979, 280-290 note 1 fig. 55 a-b, from Rās Ibn Hānī, Levant 7 1975, 104, 106 note 11 pl. 20 A-B, from the environs of Gaza (Ġazza), Tall as-Ṣāfī and Tall Ġamma. On the origin of the Cypriote Herakles and his identification with the Phoenician god Melqart, the Baᶜal ("Lord") of Tyre, see ML II 2, 2650-2652, Myres, Handbook of the Cesnola Collection, 126 and 170, Sūkās VI, 67-68.

▷

▷

71. Female head

The hair is smooth or concealed by part of a cloak or by a veil and covers the ears. White limestone with light grey patina. Recut below with a tenon to be placed in a modern base. H. 0.043 m.

Inv.No. 2125. Provenience: the environs of Ioppe (Yāfā). Acquired 1883 from Valdemar Lausen, M.D. – Den kgl. Antiksamling, Haandkatalog[4], Copenhagen 1884, 18 No. 35, NMFührer[3], Copenhagen 1908, 68 No. 5, NMVAntiksamlingen[3], Copenhagen 1918, 72 No. 5,.

For the smooth hair, cp. BMSculpture I 2, 133, C 413 fig. 211. For the face, cp. SCE III 57-59 pl. 18.2-3, from Kition, style III A.

72. Female head

The hair is hanging in a broad mass down the nape. Over the forehead a diadem, summarily rendered. White limestone with light greyish patina. Fracture below with a modern pin-hole. The tip of the nose is missing; some scratches. H. 0.060 m.

Inv.No. ABb 242. Provenience: Kition. Acquired 1853 from Henry Christy, London.

Probably part of a figure like SIMA 20.9 1984, 34 No. 113, 91, from Idalion, cf. ClRh 6/7 1932/3, 284 fig. 7, from Kameiros. Related to Nos. 55 and 60, parallels to which have been given above, i.a. from Kition. For the facial features, cp. SCE III 599-600 pl. 208, from Arsos, style V.

73. Standing beardless man

The arms hang down along the sides with the hands clenched. The hair hangs in a broad mass of beaded locks down the nape; over the forehead it is arranged in a thick mass stylized as several horizontal ranges of waves or beads; on the crown of the head the hair is radially striated. Around the hair a wreath of erect leaves. The man wears a long beltless dress, probably a wide tunic, covering the arms to the elbows. On the front the dress has many incisions, some of which form figures, e.g. two palm branches and a star below. Incisions apparently indicate the delineation of the borders at the neck, and sandal straps are likewise rendered by incised crosses on each foot. Small plinth rounded in front with sloping upper side. The rear-side of the figure is flat. White limestone with light grey to drab-coloured patina. The back, the left upper arm and the front of the plinth have been damaged by blows, and there are some cracks and scratches in addition. H. 0.422 m.

Inv.No. 3729. Provenience: unknown. Acquired 1891 from Julien Gréau's Collection in Paris. – Collection J. Gréau, Catalogue des terres-cuites grecques, vases peints et marbres antiques, Paris 1891, 267-268 No. 1261, NMFührer[3], Copenhagen 1908, 75-76 No. 11, NMVAntiksamlingen[3], Copenhagen 1918, 80 No. 11.

The type is a precursor of a Classical one, BMSculpture I 2, 64, C 159 fig. 100, but otherwise related to the types ibid. 27-28, C 33-35 figs. 28-30, 51-52, C 109-112 figs. 71-74, from different Cypriote localities. It seems to have been exported to Phoenicia, BMSculpture I 2, 86, C 215, from Ar-Rū'ād (Arados). Compare also SCE III 59-60 pl. 32.3-4, and for the wreath of leaves, ibid. pl. 31.3, from Kition, style IV A, RDAC 1978, 160, 184 pl. 24.17, from Kazaphane near Kyreneia, and BMus-Beyr 8 1946-48 pl. 33, from ᶜAmrīt (Marathos). For the modelling of the face, see SCE III 57-59 pl. 18.4-5, from Kition, style III A.

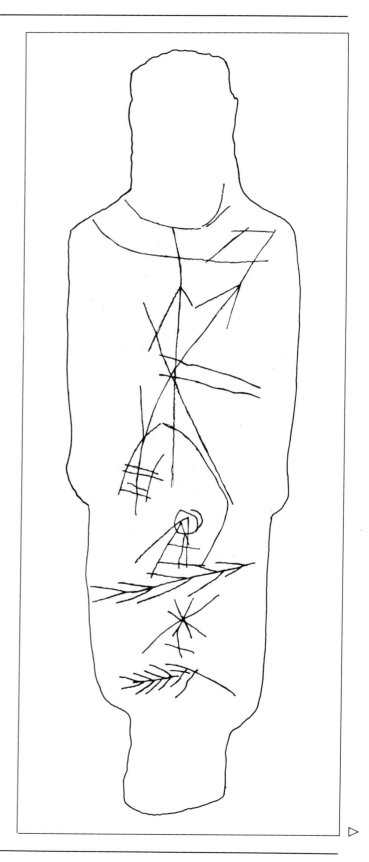

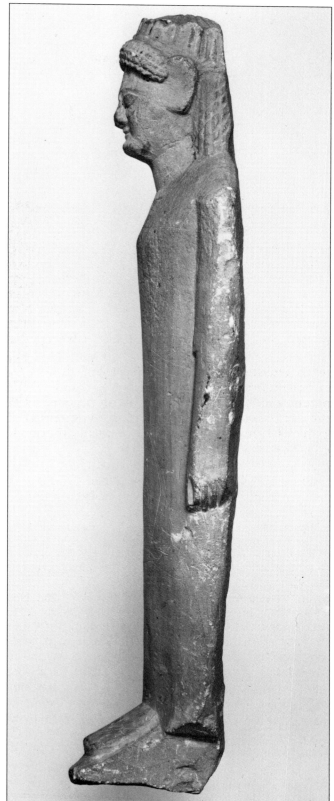

74. Standing woman

The right hand is held in front of the chest and holds a fruit or an egg. The left arm hangs down at the side with the hand clenched. The hair is hanging down in short, thick, vertical locks over the forehead and thick twisted locks down the nape. There seem to be ear ornaments on the upper part of the ear. Around the neck a tight necklace consists of three strings of beads connected in front with a four-sided spacer, while there are also two loosely hanging strings of beads with a pendant in front. The woman wears a long beltless dress, probably a wide tunic, covering the arms to the wrist. A small rectangular plinth with sloping upper side. The back of the figure is flat. White limestone with light greyish patina. Remains of red colour on the lips and on the right side of the bosom. Traces of light blue paint, probably secondary, on the upper right side of the hair. Insignificant marks of blows and scratches. H. 0.206 m.

Inv.No. 697. Provenience: Cyprus. Acquired 1872 from a dealer in Paris.
   Cp. BMSculpture I 2, 100, C 263 fig. 168, 105, C 278-279 fig. 175, from grave 16 at Salamis and grave 256 at Amathous. For the facial features, see SCE III 57-59 pls. 16.4 and 25.6, from Kition, style III A-B.   ▷

EARLY CLASSICAL

C. 475-400 B.C.

The objects described in this section, Nos. 75-76, both have their stylistic antecedents in Attic art of the Early Classical period[129]. No. 75 may still be called Epi-Archaic[130], whereas No. 76 obviously is a real Classical work[131]. The Swedish discoveries of sculpture in Cyprus make it evident that the local development of style in the 5th century B.C. was unable to keep pace at all closely with the leading Attic movements[132]. No. 76 may therefore very well belong to the second half of the century.

75. Female head

The hair is parted in the middle and falls in a wavy mass down over temples and ears; on the crown of the head, on the nape and the sides, it is covered by part of a cloak or veil hanging down over the shoulders. Flat back. White limestone with light greyish patina. Broken off below; in the fracture a modern pin-hole. Crown of head, forehead, nose, lips, chin and right side of the cloak or veil are damaged. H. 0.054 m.

Inv.No. 2126. Provenience: the environs of Ioppe (Yāfā). Acquired 1883 from Valdemar Lausen, M.D. – Den kgl. Antiksamling, Haandkatalog[4], Copenhagen 1884, 18 no. 35, NMFührer[3], Copenhagen 1908, 68 No. 5, NMVAntiksamlingen[3], Copenhagen 1918, 72 No. 5.

The type is related to the heads of seated figures like BMSculpture I 2, 134-135, C 420 fig.212 and to our No. 71 above. Same modelling of face: SCE III 265-266 pl. 58.3, from Bounoi (Vouni), style II B. Compare also RDAC 1978, 175-176 Nos. 9-10 pl. 29.1 and 3, from Pyla north-east of Kition.

76. Head of enthroned woman

The hair is parted in the middle and falls in a wavy mass down over temples and ears; on the crown and at the sides it is covered by part of a cloak or veil hanging down over the shoulders. Behind there are the remains of a tall throne-back. White limestone with light yellowish patina. A broad red stripe on the hem of the cloak or veil; there is also red on the lips, and remains of red colour on the neck indicate either a necklace or the border of a dress. There are also remains of red colour on the throne-back over the left shoulder. The upper edge of the throne is missing; crown of head, forehead, nose and chin are damaged. H. 0.044 m.

Inv.No. 2126. Provenience: the environs of Ioppe (Yāfā). Acquired 1883 from Valdemar Lausen, M.D. – Den kgl. Antiksamling, Haandkatalog[4], Copenhagen 1884, 18 No. 35, NMFührer[3], Copenhagen 1908, 68 No. 5, NMVAntiksamlingen[3], Copenhagen 1918, 72 No. 5.

Same type: BMSculpture I 2, 134-135, C 418 and C 420 fig. 212; for stripes on the chair-back see also ibid. 135, C 419 fig. 213. Closely related to our No. 75 above, but later, cp. SCE III 590 pl. 193.5 from Arsos, style VII.

LATE CLASSICAL

4th century B.C.

No. 78 is the earliest of the three specimens under this heading; it reflects the ordinary Attic style at the beginning of the 4th century B.C.[133]. No. 77 is a rather crude work. It is obvious, however, that No. 79 betrays Praxitelan influence[134]; with its soft features, which allow us to feel the approach of Hellenistic times, No. 79 is not far from the following group.

77. Standing beardless man

The right is the supporting leg, the left knee being slightly bent. The upper part of the body is bare, the lower part and the legs are concealed by a cloak passing over the left arm, which is held slightly forward. The left hand holds a bird by its wings. The right hand grasps the cloak at the waist. On the left foot incised parallel lines crossing each other indicate sandal-straps. Irregularly rounded plinth with sloping upper side. The back of the figure is crudely carved. White limestone with light yellowish patina. Red colour is used for the cloak, also on the back, for the nipples, and on the upper part of the plinth; the eyes of the bird are marked by a red circle, and on its body there are red dots to indicate the legs. A broad bluish black stripe on the man's chest and shoulders may represent some kind of ornament or amulet band.

Instead of the original head, which is missing, a similar head of the same stone has been attached to the torso. The hair is parted at the crown of the head and arranged in a thick, curly or wavy mass over forehead and nape. Around the hair a wreath of leaves. Red colour is used for the lips. On the left side of the neck a reddish brown stripe (traces of rust?). Insignificant damage. H. with disassociate head 0.185 m.

Inv.No. 699. Provenience: Cyprus. Acquired 1872 from a dealer in Paris.

A related figure type: BMSculpture I 2, 69, C 173-174 fig. 108. For the head, cp. SCE III 382-383 pl. 133.8, from Mersinaki, style IV A. The bird is probably a dove, cf. Atlas of the Cesnola Collection I pls. 114.814-815 and 116.842. The head of a related figure, presumably a local North-Phoenician production influenced from Cyprus, was discovered in the Harbour Sanctuary at Sūkās, Sūkās VI, 33-35 No. 2 figs. 99-100, and is somewhat later than its Cypriote models, which belong to the time c. 475-425 B.C.

▷

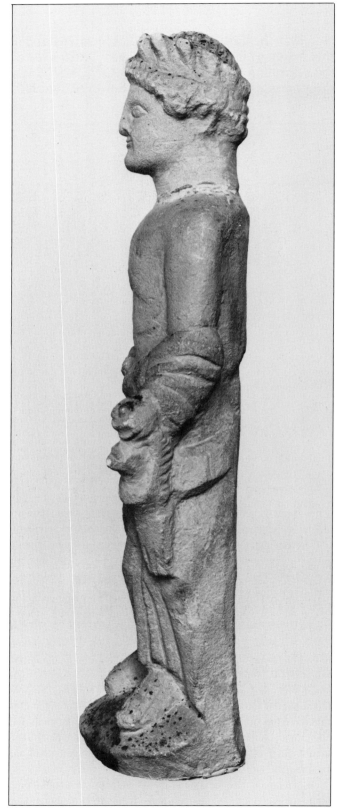

78. Female head

The hair, which seems to have been gathered in a knot or the like at the nape, is covered on the crown of the head, the nape and the sides by part of a cloak or a veil, which hangs down over the shoulders, but leaves the hair free at the forehead and the temples. The triangular neck-opening of a dress is indicated by incision. White limestone with light grey patina. On the lips and front edge of the veil traces of red colour; greyish blue traces on the veil. Broken off below, in the fracture a modern pin-hole. The front edge of the cloak or veil and the tip of the nose have been damaged. H. 0.058 m.

Inv.No. ABb 242. Provenience: Kition. Acquired 1853 from Henry Christy, London.

Part of a figure like SCE III 60 pl. 35.4, from Kition, style V. Same type of head: ibid. 590-591 pls. 194-196, from Arsos, style VIII. The facial features remind one of the head ibid. 382-383 pl. 133.11, from Mersinaki, style IV A.

79. Female head

The hair, which seems to have been gathered in a knot at the lower part of the nape, is covered on the crown of the head, the nape and the sides by part of a cloak or veil, which hangs down over the shoulders, but leaves the hair at the forehead and temples free as well as the ears with their ornaments. White limestone with light grey patina. Broken off below; in the fracture a modern tenon-hole. The hair on the forehead, the left part of the face, nose, lips, chin and front edge of the cloak or veil are damaged. H. 0.113 m.

Inv.No. ABb 242. Provenience: Kition. Acquired 1853 from Henry Christy, London.

Same type as No. 78; but the execution is more detailed and in some points different, cp. SCE III 592-594 pl. 199, from Arsos, style IX, which is, however, clearly later. The ear-ornaments, the left one the more distinct, seem to have been intended to represent specimens of the type K. Hadaczek, Der Ohrschmuck der Griechen und Etrusker, Vienna 1903, 46-49 figs. 86-89, BMJewellery 184 fig. 60 No. 1684-1685 pl. 31, R.A. Higgins, Greek and Roman Jewellery, London 1961, 161-164.

HELLENISTIC

3rd-1st centuries B.C.

The crude execution of the Hellenistic specimens makes it difficult to form a safe impression of their models. However, the style is chronologically well defined through the Swedish finds in Cyprus, and to all appearances Nos. 80-84 belong to the earlier part of the period. Nos. 82-84 continue the trend which, among our Classical Cypriote sculptures, is represented by No. 78, whereas Nos. 80-81 are Epi-Praxitelan, cf. No. 79. The summary carving, which allows eyebrows and nose, and their shadows, alone to express the face, was probably an impressionistic attempt to render the richly varied contrasts of light and shade which characterize many Hellenistic marble heads.

---

80. Standing woman

The left is the supporting leg, the right knee being slightly bent and advanced. The woman wears a long dress, which leaves the arms bare, and over it a cloak (himation?), which passes under the right arm and over the head, and hangs down over the left arm and side. The right arm is lowered; the hand seems to hold a fruit or the like. The left hand is raised in front of the shoulder and grasps the hem of the cloak. The rear is flat. White limestone with light gray to drab-coloured patina. On the back of the figure, there are remains of stucco on the cloak's lower seam, and on the cloak itself there are many traces of light blue and light green paint, probably secondary; the lower border is – perhaps likewise secondarily – painted black. The lower part of the figure from under the knees and most of the left hand are missing; there is minor damage in addition. H. 0.390 m.

Inv.No. ABb 241. Provenience: Kition. Acquired 1853 from Henry Christy, London.
Same motif: Atlas of the Cesnola Collection I pl. 94.630, from Golgoi. Related: BMSculpture I 2, 121, C 360 fig. 194, cp. also our Nos. 78-79 above. For the face: SCE III 526 pl. 160.2, from Soloi, style I A, and ibid. 593 pl. 199.7, from Arsos, style IX. No. 80, however, is inferior to these both in workmanship and in degree of preservation. ▷

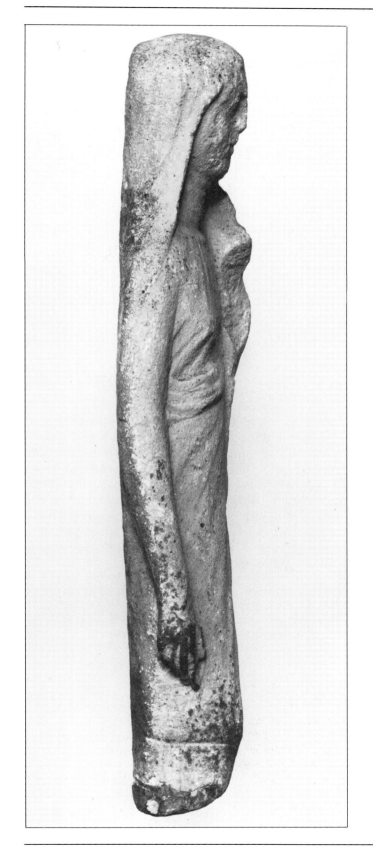

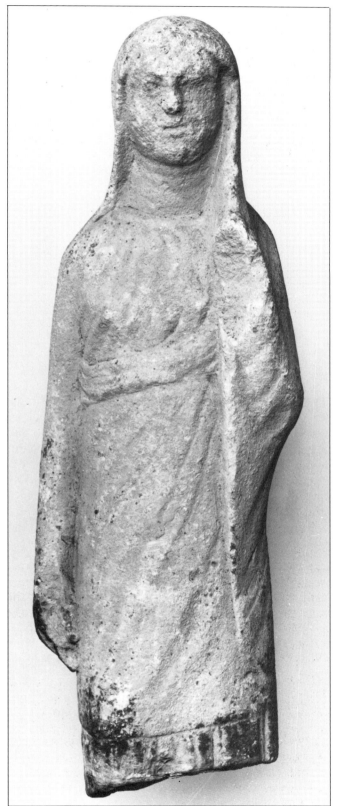

81. Female head

The hair is parted in the middle and combed back from the temples; it is partly covered by a cloak or veil, which is hanging down over the shoulders, and around it there is a wreath of leaves. The ears seem to have pyramid-shaped pendants, which, however, are carved in one with the cloak or veil. The back is flat. White limestone with light yellowish to grey patina. On the cloak or veil remains of red colour. Broken off below. The right half of the wreath is missing. H. 0.066 m.

Inv.No. 2127. Provenience: the environs of Ioppe (Yāfā). Acquired 1883 from Valdemar Lausen, M.D. – Den kgl. Antiksamling, Haandkatalog[4], Copenhagen 1884, 18 No. 35, NMFührer[3], Copenhagen 1908, 68 No. 5, NMVAntiksamlingen[3], Copenhagen 1918, 72. No. 5.

Close parallels were found at Idalion, SIMA 20.9 1984, 45 Nos. 173-174, 100. A figure with a similar head, but of unknown provenience: BMSculpture I 2, 113-114, C 327 fig. 183. Same type of head: SCE II 791 pl. 240.2, from Hagia Eirene, style III, and SCE III 593 pl. 200.7, from Arsos, style IX. The summary carving of the face recurs both on the quoted specimen from Hagia Eirene and on another from the same site, SCE II 791 pl. 240.3, style III, as well as on a head from Arsos, SCE III 593 pl. 200.5, style IX. For the pyramid-shaped ear-ornaments, see Hadaczek, op.cit. 27-31 figs. 48-55 and Higgins, op.cit. 165-166.

82. Female head

The head seems slightly turned towards the right. The hair is parted in the middle and forms a thick mass over the forehead, from which is has been combed back. The hair is partly covered by a cloak or veil, which is hanging down over the shoulders, and around it there is a wreath of erect leaves. The back is flat. White limestone with light grey patina. Broken off below; in the fracture a modern pin-hole. A piece of the back and the left side is missing. H. 0.058 m.

Inv.No. ABb 242. Provenience: Kition. Acquired 1853 from Henry Christy, London.

For parallels see SIMA 20.9 1984, 48 Nos. 190-191, 103-104, from Idalion, and No. 81 above.

83. Female head

The hair is parted in the middle and combed back from the temples, and is partly covered by a cloak or veil with deeply incised lines indicating the folds on both sides of the head. Eyes and mouth are not rendered by carving, but must have been painted. Flat back. White limestone with lime incrustations and a light grey patina. H. 0.082 m.

Inv.No. ABb 242. Provenience: Kition. Acquired 1853 from Henry Christy, London.
   For parallels, see SIMA 20.9 1984, 48-49 Nos. 194-195, 104, from Idalion, and Nos. 80-81 above.

84. Female head

The back, the edge of the cloak or veil at the left side of the head, and the neck are missing. The surface much weathered. H. 0.082 m.

Inv.No. ABb 242. Provenience: Kition. Acquired 1853 from Henry Christy, London.

A separate class of sculptures like the Hellenized Cypriote, Etruscan and Northwest Indian is formed by those works which were made by emigrant Greek settlers on the Phoenician coast and their local followers. Archaeological excavations have proved that the first Greek factories there were founded in the late 9th and 8th century B.C., and that the settlements achieved their greatest prosperity in the 6th century[135]. As far as stone sculpture is concerned it seems that Greek workshops were established in the regions dominated by the Phoenician kings of Arados and Sidon about 480 and 465 B.C. respectively[136].

That also this class of sculpture is represented in the Museum is due to the growth of interest in the archaeology of the Levant beginning in the late 19th century, an interest aroused by the acquisitions from the Danish vice-consul J. Løytved in Beirut[137], by J. Østrup's explorations in the Syrian desert[138], and, in this century, by the Danish excavations in Shiloh, Palmyra, Ḥamā and Tall Sūkās.

85. Mummy-shaped sarcophagus

The coffin proper has a flat bottom, a block-shaped foot-piece and sides tapering slightly downward, which reproduce the contours of a mummy with head, shoulders, thighs and calves indicated. The hollow inside of the coffin also has the contours of a mummy. The contours of the back of the trunk and legs are indicated along the sides by means of a rough dressing of the bottom edge, a dressing which continues as a broad band around the lower edge of the head-piece and on the left side of the foot-piece. The underside of the bottom is not quite plane, but has a concave portion roughly corresponding to the lower half of the mummy, from buttocks to heels.

The domed lid has the same mummy-contours as the coffin and a corresponding foot-piece, large, pentagonal and slightly concave, with broad vertical sides and a top of two surfaces meeting in an obtuse angle like a ridge-roof. The head-piece is shaped as a beardless face surrounded by a thick mass of curly hair along the forehead and the temples; the curls are rendered as four rows of big knobs. The facial outline is egg-shaped, tapering downward with a faintly smiling mouth, a long straight nose, slightly slanting eyes with large medial commissures, and ears obliquely set and turned outward in the Egyptian way. On the sides of the lid there are three lifting-lugs, each c. 0.14-0.15 m long, one under the crown of the head, one near the right shoulder, and one low down on the foot-piece; near the left shoulder there are moreover traces of a fourth lifting-lug, which has been removed.

On the coffin and lifting-lugs are clear traces of working with toothed chisel and rasp. The interior of the lid is roughly worked with a pick, and the interior of the coffin with a toothed chisel. On the left exterior side of the head-piece, both on the coffin and on the lid, a cross $+$ is incised with the vertical bar almost continuous from lid to coffin; the same is found on the exterior of the foot-piece. These signs are either simple marks of congruity or the letter "taw". Near the edge of the coffin, at the left shoulder, there are other incised signs: $\vee$ $/$ possibly the remains of a letter, "šin", "sigma" or "mu"; a few short, incised strokes on the corresponding part of the lid may perhaps be explained in the same way. Coarse-grained white marble with yellowish grey to reddish yellow patina; in the incisions also remains of ancient patina. The head-piece of the lid has been broken off, but reattached to the lid. The tip of the nose, the lifting lugs and the edges have been damaged by blows, and the surface has a number of scratches, partly modern. The upper edge of the coffin is also rather damaged. Horizontal lime deposits along the interior edge may be a consequence of water collecting in the coffin while it was standing in the tomb. Blackish grey spots on edges and interior are probably partly due to modern re-employment. H. 0.79 m, of coffin alone 0.41 m, of lid 0.39 m. L. 2.30 m, W. 0.86 m. The width of the coffin's edge is 0.08-0.09 m, at the foot-piece 0.105 m, with an offset to hold the lid 0.015 m high and 0.030-0.035 m wide. A corresponding recess 0.04-0.05 m wide is found on the edges of the lid.

▷

Inv.No. 13431. Provenience: Antarados (Ṭarṭūs). Acquired 1953 from the Ny Carlsberg Foundation. – Weltkunst 24/9, Munich 1954, 11, E. Kukahn, Anthropoïde Sarkophage in Beyrouth und die Geschichte dieser sidonischen Sarkophagkunst, Berlin 1955, 87 No. 2 (the provenience erroneously given as "Latakya-Banyas"), NMArb 1958, 34-36 fig. 3, M.-L. Buhl, The Late Egyptian Anthropoid Stone Sarcophagi, Copenhagen 1959, 185, IV c, 189 fig. 92, 193, ActaArch 35 1964, 67 fig. 7, 71, 76, NMVÆgypten og Vestasien, Copenhagen 1968, 56 No. 10, Guides to the Danish National Museum, Egypt and Western Asia, Copenhagen 1968, 56 No. 10, M.-L. Buhl, A Hundred Masterpieces from the Ancient Near East in the National Museum of Denmark and the History of its Ancient Near Eastern Collections, Copenhagen 1974, 88 No. 77, 91, 122 note 139, Atti del I° Congresso Internazionale di Studi Fenici e Punici I, Rome 1983, 201 pl. 49.2, Études Chypriotes 9 1987, 60 note 50, ActaArch. 58 1987, 217-219 fig. 11, Iranica Antiqua 23 1988, 289-290.

Other anthropoid marble sarcophagi are said also to have come from Antarados (Ṭarṭūs) or the area between this town and Marathos (ᶜAmrīt), Buhl, Sarcophagi 182, II a-b, 184, III l and q, 188 Nos. 11-12. The town of Antarados seems to have come into existence no earlier than the Roman period, but we must assume that Arados (Ar-Rū'ād) had its cemeteries, for which there was no room in the island city itself, in the area just mentioned, where Strabo records the harbour town of Enhydra (Tall Ġamqā) at a river-mouth 2 kms. south of Tartūs, G. Saadé, Histoire de Lattaquié I, Damas 1964, 102-103, J.-P. Rey-Coquais, Arados et sa pérée, Paris 1974, 208-209, 10-11, 65, 141, carte 1. As regards shape and style, our sarcophagus is rather closely connected with those found at Sidon, which are usually held to have been made in a local Greek workshop. The obvious Greek parallels to the head on No. 85 are different Epi-Archaic products of the years around 460 B.C., all of them provincial, e.g. Buhl, Sarcophagi 185, IV b 2, 186, IV h and V a, 188 No. 2, 189 No. 16, HdArch III 1, Munich 1950, 112 pl. 35.4, B. Ashmole, Late Archaic and Early Classical Greek Sculpture in Sicily and South Italy, London 1935, 26 pls. 15.66 and 18.74, L. Quarles van Ufford, Les terres-cuites siciliennes, Assen 1941, 108 note 3, 131 fig. 66, 131, 133 note 1 fig. 67. No. 85 was thus probably carved by a Greek sculptor in Sidon at about this date, by order of some outstanding person in Arados, for a tomb on the mainland coast in the environs of the Aradian port of Enhydra. The removal of the lifting-lug on the left side and of most of the rough edge-dressing of the foot-piece on the same side shows that the sarcophagus was placed in the tomb with its left side visible. The lavish use of the toothed chisel does not necessarily indicate Greek work, as this technique has been documented in the Near East as early as the 13th and following centuries B.C., Lachish 5, Tel Aviv 1975, 38-40 pls. 10.4-5 and 11 (otherwise: C. Nylander, Ionians in Pasargadae, Uppsala 1970, 53-56 note 125). ▷

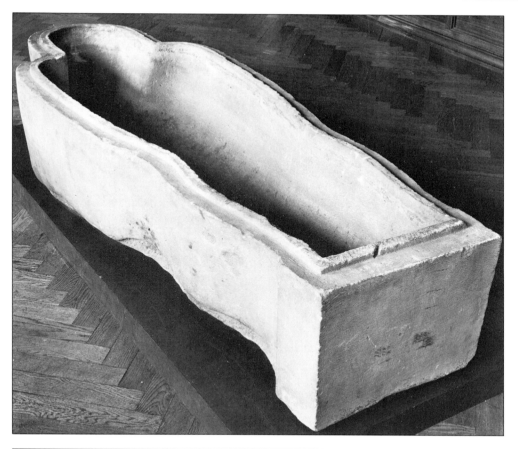

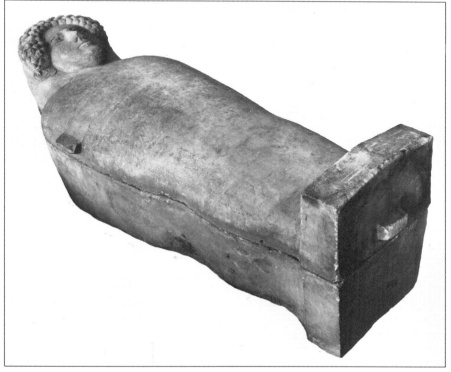

86. Upper part of relief stela with rounded top

On the front a representation in very low relief: above, in the rounded part, a winged sun-disc flanked by uraei. The wings of the sun-disc have a double row of feathers, but they are not parted in the middle. The uraei have an indistinct object placed on top of their heads, either the Egyptian double crown or a small sun-disc. Below, a woman facing left with her face in profile and the bust in three-quarter view. The face has a straight nose, deeply set eyes, and a heavy jaw. The wavy hair is gathered at the back of the crown in a small bunch fastened by a narrow band. The woman is wearing a tunic and over it a cloak covering the left shoulder and passing under the right arm. On her right shoulder a spindle-shaped object, probably the pointed button of a brooch or pin. Her right, rather crudely carved hand is raised in a gesture of adoration with the palm turned outward; a thick fillet is tied around the wrist and is hanging down along the arm. The left arm is lowered obliquely forwards. The edges of the stela are smoothly dressed, but the back has been left coarsely carved. Medium-grained whitish grey marble with a light grey, slightly brownish patina. There are a number of minor marks of blows and scratches on the surface. Most of the right wing and of the right uraeus as well as the entire lower part of the stela including the elbows and the left under-arm of the figure are missing. H. 0.230 m. W. 0.170 m. D. 0.072 m.

Inv.No. 14384. Provenience: unknown. Acquired 1961 from a private collector in Copenhagen.

It has been suggested that this fragment had been found in the region of Tyre, where similar commemorative stelae, particularly those of Isibarak, daughter of Eshmunshamar, and of Baᶜalshamar, son of ᶜAbdosir, were dug up at Umm al-ᶜAwāmīd, M. Dunand & R. Duru, Oumm el-ᶜAmed, Paris 1962, 163 No. 1, 191 No. 11 pl. 84.3, 165 No. 9, 194 No. 16 pl. 88bis.1, Atti del Iº Congresso .. di Studi Fenici .. I, Rome 1983, 172 pl.

28.1. Monuments of the same kind, however, did also exist elsewhere in Phoenicia, for example in the sanctuary of Eshmun at Bustān aš-Šaiḥ near Sidon and in the island city of Arados, Renan, Mission de Phénicie, 29 No. 7 pl. 4.5, Au Pays de Baal et d'Astarté, 10000 ans d'art en Syrie, Petit Palais, Paris 1983, 226 No. 257, Berytus I 1934, 45-46 pl. 12, N. Jidejian, Sidon, Beirut 1971, 58 fig. 181, and all of them, of course, derive from stelae like the famous one from Nahr al-ᶜAbrāš near ancient Simyra (not found at ᶜAmrīt or Marathos as often stated), H. Bossert, Altsyrien, Tübingen 1951, 34 No. 498 pl. 152, Au Pays de Baal et d'Astarté, 222-223 No. 255. Whereas the Umm al-ᶜAwāmīd stelae are made of the local limestone, the material of those from Sidon and Arados is marble. The specimen from Sidon is clearly Pre-Hellenistic, but the Aradian fragment must probably be placed in the late 4th century B.C. This latter and Isibarak's monument, both with representations of women, are the nearest parallels to No. 86, which seems to take an intermediate position. The drapery of Isibarak shows great resemblance to the himatia of the so-called Herculanians and related works of the period 340-280 B.C., HdArch III 1, Munich 1950, 242 pl. 86.1-2, 301 pl. 107.2; but according to Dunand language, style and lettering of the inscription speak for a date in the first half of the 2nd century B.C., op.cit. 194-195. The stone was perhaps carved earlier, the monument kept in store, and the inscription added after purchase. The hair of the woman on No. 86 recalls a fashion of the later part of the 5th century B.C. and most of the 4th, e.g. HdArch III 1, 195 pl. 72.1, C. Picard, Manuel d'Archéologie grecque, la Sculpture IV 2.1, Paris 1954, 243-247 fig. 103. There is scarcely reason to place the National Museum's fragment much later that the late 4th or the early 3rd century B.C. The spindle-shaped object on the right shoulder should be compared with the pear or apple finials of certain Greek pins of a type occurring at least from the 7th to the 3rd century B.C., which is also represented on Cyprus, P. Jacobsthal, Greek Pins, Oxford 1956, 28-29 figs. 115, 117, 120, 121 and 123, 34-37 figs. 133, 137 and 143, 82-83 fig. 314, cf. 108-109 figs. 335 and 338, 186 figs. 612 and 613.

1. K. Bittel. Prähistorische Forschung in Kleinasien, IstForsch 6 1934, 37, cf. 95-103, 115-118, Archaeologia 87 1937, 268, AJA 73 1969, 27-29, 31-32, O. Höckmann in Thimme, 159-167, 178-189.
2. NMArb 1970, 57-58.
3. BSA 63 1968, 47-48 and AJA 73 1969, 21.
4. MémSocAntN 1896, 15; for the stone carving see JHS 50 1930, 319, 324, S. Casson, The Technique of Early Greek Sculpture, Oxford 1933, 15-23, P. Getz-Preziosi in Thimme, 74-93 and E. Oustinoff in Cycladiaca, 38-43, observations based on practical experiments.
5. A. Evans, The Palace of Minos I, London 1921, 48 fig. 13, AntK 8 1965, 81-83, AJA 73 1969, 28 fig. 4.
6. MémSocAntN 1896, 12-14, Evans, op.cit. 51, AJA 73 1969, 31-32, Höckmann, op.cit. 160-161, see, however, also REA 32 1930, 99.
7. Cf. C. Doumas, The N.P. Goulandris Collection of Early Cycladic Art, Athens 1968, 88-94.
8. Phylakopi 194-195, C. Renfrew, in An Island Polity: The Archaeology of Exploitation in Melos, eds. C. Renfrew and M. Wagstaff, Cambridge 1982, 37, AntK 8 1965, 78 note 23: uncertain if in cultic contexts. E. Schofield has assigned three fragmentary Early Cycladic marble figurines found in Late Bronze Age levels at Keos to a shrine, a Late Bronze Age ritual context within House A, see Davis, Discussion in Cycladiaca, 31. Up to August 1974 43 fragments of marble figurines had been found in the settlement area of Hagia Eirene on Keos, Hesperia 40 1971, 113-127, 43 1974, 77-79; furthermore a fragmentary marble figurine was found in the settlement at Hagios Kosmas, House E, G.E. Mylonas, Hagios Kosmas, Princeton 1959, 29 no. 7 pl. 163. That the figures found in settlements should be stray finds from workshops has been rejected by Renfrew, in Cycladiaca, 25, who argues for the use of the figurines in domestic cults, op.cit. 27-29.
9. AM 16 1891, 46.
10. MémSocAntN 1896, 14-15, BMSculpture I 1, 4, REA 32 1930, 101, Wiesner, GuJ, 172-173, Hesperia 40 1971, 125, Renfrew in Thimme, 70, SIMA 48 1977, 62-63, Renfrew in Cycladiaca, 26. This possibility has lately been analysed by J.L. Davis in Cycladiaca, 17-20, who is against such an assumption. See also P. Getz-Preziosi, MetrMusJ 16 1982, 5-32.
11. The very large idols have particularly been found at Amorgos and were perhaps originally cult objects, AntK 8 1965, 78-79, Renfrew in Cycladiaca, 29. No marble figures have, however, been discovered in the excavation of the supposed Early Cycladic sanctuary at Korphe t'Aroniou at Naxos.
12. See also AntK 8 1965, 80 note 31, 81.
13. AntK 8 1965, 78 note 3, 80.
14. MémSocAntN 1896, 12-14, REA 32 1930, 97-105, Wiesner, GuJ, 172.
15. Schmidt, SS, 277-280, Dörpfeld, T&I, 379-383.
16. Dörpfeld, T&I, 382.
17. AJA 38 1934, 230, 233, Troy II, 227-229, cf. U. Bahadir Alkim, Anatolien I, Geneva 1968, 250-251.
18. Troy I, 27-28, 44-46 fig. 127.
19. Alkim, loc.cit.
20. AJA 73 1969, 4 fig. 1, 27.
21. AJA 84 1980, 155.
22. AJA 73 1969, 3 note 17, 28 fig. 4.
23. AJA 73 1969, 9, 13, and 3 note 17, 28 fig. 4, C. Renfrew, The Emergence of Civilisation, London 1972, 220-222.
24. Cf. BSA 66 1971, 57-78
25. Xanthoudides, 21-22: No. 124 from Tholos A, Nos. 125 and 127 from Tholos B, No. 126 from Tomb Γ, No. 122 from AB, the room between the tomb buildings A, B and E, AJA 73 1969, 7 fig. 2 IV E, 19 IV E 2, 3, 4, 5, 20 IV

F 27 pl. 4 c, BSA 66 1971, 63.

26. Xanthoudides, 121: No. 224 from AB, AJA 73 1969, 19 IV E 6, BSA 66 1971, 63.
27. Xanthoudides, 92; at Koumasa Middle Minoan I pottery was found outside all the tholoi, ibid. 42-45, and a single piece from Koumasa's tholos B may also possibly date from Middle Minoan I, ibid. 13-14 No. 8 a 4156 pls. 5 and 20.
28. AJA 73 1969, 19 IV 12-14, BSA 66 1971, 63.
29. R. Dussaud, Les civilisations préhellénistiques, Paris 1914, 345 fig. 252, REA 32 1930, 101 fig. 1, AA 1937, 256, Wiesner, GuJ, 172 note 4.
30. Palace of Minos, Index, London 1936, 182 ad I 122 fig. 167 and IV 210 fig. 162.
31. AJA 38 1934, 275-276 fig. 21, Mylonas, Hagios Kosmas, 75, 77, 80-85, 87, AJA 73 1969, 14 VI 13-14, 20 IV F 28.
32. C. Blegen, Zygouries, Cambridge, Mass. 1928, 194 fig. 183, AJA 73 1969, 11 note 41.
33. Blegen, op.cit. 3.
34. Thimme, 427-428 cat.nos. 27-28, possibly from the Makrykapa district, C.P. Calligas in Cycladiaca, 90, and 92 "Folded Arm Figurines" from the cemetery of Manika.
35. AJA 84 1980, 154.
36. Phylakopi, 194 pl. 39.3-4, AJA 73 1969, 25 Phyl. 3-4.
37. Phylakopi, 194 pl. 39.7, period II?, cf. 163, AJA 73 1969, 25 Phyl. 7.
38. Phylakopi, 195 pl. 39.2, AJA 73 1969, 25 Phyl. 2.
39. Phylakopi, 22, 195, similar to pl. 39.2, period I, AJA 73 1969, 25 Phyl 2.
40. Phylakopi, 195 pl. 39.1, AJA 73 1969, 25 Phyl. 1.
41. Hesperia 40 1971, 113-126, 43 1974, 77-79.
42. AJA 73 1969, 24-26 and 28 fig. 4.
43. So already D. Fimmen, Die kretisch-mykenische Kultur, Leipzig & Berlin 1921, 211, who nevertheless placed the lower limit of the period I too late; the Kamarais ware of Middle Minoan II provides the terminus ante quem.
44. Hesperia 40 1971, 123.
45. W.C. Cummer and E. Schofield, Keos III, Ayia Irini: House A, Mainz 1984, 140.
46. See J.L. Davis, Discussion in Cycladiaca, 31.
47. BMSculpture I 2, 2.
48. Cf. ActaArch 48 1977, 139-154, 49 1978, 239-240.
49. BMSculpture I 1, 159; G. Kaulen, Daidalika, Munich 1967, 55, cf. Nos. 16 and 42 below: "Werkstatt von Kameiros".
50. Lindos I, 403-405.
51. RDAC 1978, 120.
52. Levant 7 1975, 107, Sūkās VI, Copenhagen 1979, 14-15 No. 16 fig. 24, 33-35 Nos. 2-3 figs. 99-102, 36 No. 5 figs. 104-105, 40-41 No. 15 fig. 126, 45-46 No. 21 figs. 137-139, 51-52 No. 41 fig. 164.
53. E.g. F. Poulsen, Catalogue of Ancient Sculpture, Copenhagen 1951, 27-28, No. 10 c, from Cyprus, and Nos. 874-875, acquired in Egypt, A.M. Nielsen, in SIMA 20.8 1983, 10-11, 35-36 nos. 28, 34 and 35.
54. Among the Glypthotek's Cypriote objects Poulsen, op.cit. 24 No. 7, SIMA 20.8 1983, 13, 43 no. 47, from Paphos, is of this material.
55. Vroulia, 14 note 6.
56. National Museum, Inv.No. 11330, Vroulia, 111 No. 4 pl. 23.13 a-b.
57. BMSculpture I 1, 200, B 470-471.
58. BMSculpture I 2, 144, C 435.
59. Atlas of the Cesnola Collection I, Boston 1885 pl. 95.642: note particularly the neck and the tail.
60. SCE III, 251 pl. 76.3, found in a context of the first half of the 5th century B.C.
61. Salamine de Chypre IV, Paris 1973, 19-45 fig. 12 a-b pls. 6-8, RDAC 1978, 120.
62. Salamine de Chypre IV, 30 pl. 10 e-f.
63. E.g. SCE III, 258 pl. 76.2, from Bounoi

(Vouni), second half of the 5th century B.C.

64. SCE II, 348 pls. 66.41 and 161.4, pl. 66.42.
65. Salamine de Chypre IV, 30 pl. 10 a-b.
66. E.g. Lindos I, 346 No. 1244 pl. 55, see now V. Webb, Archaic Greek Faiences, Warminster 1978, 81, 94-96 Nos. 485-550 pl. 14, 105-107 Nos. 675-702 pls. 16-17.
67. Among them one with an Egyptian crown like certain sphinxes, Lindos I, 457 No. 1854 pl. 79.
68. AJA 78 1974, 290.
69. Salamine de Chypre IV, 45.
70. BICS 16 1969, 1, 4-5.
71. Lindos I, 402-403.
72. Naucratis II, London 1888, 67 Nos. 858 and 864(?) pl. 22, BSA 5 1898/9, 33, 56 No. 114 pl. 5, SCE IV 2, 469 note 1.
73. Athenaios, Deipnosophistai XV 657 f – 676 c.
74. Lindos I, 402.
75. ClRh 6/7 1932/3, 279-287 figs. 1-10, cf. RDAC 1978, 111 note 2, 113 note 6, 114 notes 8-9.
76. SCE IV 2, 333 fig. 5, cf. RDAC 1978, 111 note 5.
77. Délos XI, Paris 1928, 155 figs. 106-107, BSASuppl 6 1967, 181, 185 pl. 68, Samos VII, Bonn 1968, 54-146, cf. RDAC 1978, 111 notes 6-7, 115 notes 5-6.
78. L.D. Caskey, Catalogue of Greek and Roman Sculpture, Museum of Fine Arts, Boston 1925, 5-7 No. 3, cf. H. Schrader, Marmorbildwerke der Akropolis, Frankfurt 1939, 17. – Bearded head, art dealer's photo in the Ny Carlsberg Glyptothek.
79. Mission de Phénicie, Paris 1864, 56 pl. 21.3.
80. Ibid. 850-851 note ad p. 68.
81. RA 37 1879, 321-323 pl. 11, CRAI 1926, 57-58, Syria 7 1926, 420, BMusBeyr 7 1944/5, 99-107 pls. 14-29, BMusBeyr 8 1946-48, 81-107 pls. 30-42, AASyr 11/2 1961/2, 8 pl. 4.1-2.
82. BMSculpture I 2, 86, C 215.
83. AASyr 11/2 1961/2, 113-134, Sūkās VI,

Copenhagen 1979, 14-15 ad No. 16 fig. 24, 33-37 Nos. 2-3 and 5 figs. 99-102 and 104-105, 40-41 No. 15 fig. 126, 45-46 No. 21 figs. 137-139, 51-52 No. 41 fig. 164, 66-68; Syria 56 1979, 288-290 note 1 fig. 55 a-b; JHS 58 1938, 164, MN 7.
84. FdB I, 93 No. 1361 and 128 No. 1888 pl. 42.
85. SCE IV 2, 324 figs. 49-50.
86. ʿAtiqot 6/7 1966/7, 21-22, Nos. 108-118 pls. 15-16, Levant 7 1975, 104, 106 pl. 20 A-B.
87. AEphem 1899, 51-56 pl. 4.
88. Cf. ActaArch 30 1959, 147-165, J. Boardman, The Greeks Overseas², London 1980, 118-133.
89. W.B. Dinsmoor, The Architecture of Ancient Greece, London 1950, 125-126, 134.
90. Naucratis I, London 1886, 13 pl. 2.
91. Op.cit. 11-13 pl. 44.
92. The earliest Greek pottery found at Naukratis is dated about 630-620 B.C., BSA 34 1933/4, 86 note 2, Boardman op.cit. 121.
93. Naucratis II, 55-59 pls. 13-15.
94. Naucratis II, 35 pl. 3, cf. C. Weickert, Typen der archaischen Architektur, Augsburg 1929, 64 No. 5, 87, Boardman, op.cit. 119-120.
95. Naucratis II, 36, Weickert, op.cit. 129.
96. Vroulia, 89, Lindos I, 44, RDAC 1978, 111 note 2, 115 notes 3-4.
97. E.g. Vroulia 18-20 pl. 15, ActaArch 13 1942, 24-25 figs. 13-14, cf. 14-15, and Vroulia 26 pl. 14.8, 43 pl. 33 p 2, cf. H. Payne, Necrocorinthia, Oxford 1931, 281.
98. RDAC 1978, 111 note 2, 114 notes 10-12, 115 notes 1-2; the exception is a figure in the style of the 5th century B.C., from the west slope of the Acropolis, Lindos I, No. 1760 pl. 72.
99. Lindos I, 44, 512 No. 2106 pl. 95 and 564 No. 2329 pl. 109.
100. Buschor, AS II, 34-35 figs. 123, 134-135.
101. ClRh 4 1931, 391-392 No. 20 figs. 448-450, cf. P. Knoblauch, Studien zur archaischgriechischen Tonbildnerei, Bleicherode a.H.

1937, 152 No. 184; Lindos I, 507.

102. Cf. HdArch I, Munich 1939, 837.

103. Salamine de Chypre IV, 41-42.

104. SCE IV 2, 451, 467, 471.

105. Sūkās VI, Copenhagen 1979, 14-15 No. 16 fig. 24.

106. SCE II, 820, SCE III, 71-72, 264-265, 288-289, 393-398, 539, 585-594, AA 1936, 571-578, SCE IV, 92-124.

107. RDAC 1978, 112-118.

108. AJA 78 1974, 287.

109. BSASuppl 6 1967, 181, 185 Nos. 1-2 pl. 68.

110. Samos VII, Bonn 1968, 82, C 175 pl. 115; 72, C 80 and C 83 pl. 112, C 121 pl. 97 and C 126 pl. 109.

111. E.g. Kaulen, op.cit. 129, where our Nos. 16 and 42 are placed in the third and fifth Dedalic groups respectively, i.e. c. 660-650 and c. 640-620 B.C.

112. Cf. Buschor, AS I, 9 figs. 5-10.

113. Buschor, AS II, 33 fig. 115, NCGColl 2 1938, 81, 85-87 figs. 15-16, Richter, Kouroi, 82 No. 66 figs. 221-223.

114. Buschor, AS 11, 26-27 figs. 90-91, BMSculpture I 1, 103-112 pls. 6-15, IstForsch 27 1970, 71-93 pls. 40-62.

115. Atlas of the Cesnola Collection I, pl. 95.641-642, Salamine de Chypre IV, 32-33 fig. 14.

116. Cf. the Corinthian development from works like Payne, op.cit. 171 fig. 73 to the figure ibid. 173 fig. 76, and from pl. 50.1 to 50.4.

117. E.g. Buschor, AS I, 12-13 figs. 29 and 36, II, 24-25 figs. 80 and 83.

118. Cp. our No. 16 and Buschor, AS I, 9 figs. 5-6.

119. Buschor, AS I, 12-13 figs. 30 and 33.

120. Buschor, AS III, 48 fig. 178,

121. Buschor, AS II, 26-27 figs. 92-95, 32 figs. 112-114, V, 84-86 figs. 345-350.

122. Cp. Nos. 62, 63 and 66 with Buschor, AS II, 26-27 fig. 90, 39 fig. 137, BMSculpture I 1, 104, 106-107, B 271-272 pls. 6-7.

123. BMSculpture I 1, 112-113, B 281 pl. 16.

124. Buschor, AS II, 35 fig. 130.

125. Buschor, AS I, 13 fig. 35.

126. E.g. Buschor, AS I, 13 fig. 35, and II, 35 fig. 133.

127. Op.cit. II, 35 fig. 133, III, 53 fig. 196.

128. Cf. H. Payne & G.M. Young, Archaic Marble Sculpture from the Acropolis, London 1936, 38-42 pls. 80 and 82, Schrader, Marmorbildwerke, 104-106 No. 55 pls. 78-81, 61-62 No. 20 pl. 29.

129. Cf. ActaArch 8 1937, 57 fig. 36, 59.

130. Cf. Payne & Young, op.cit. 34-35 pl. 77, Schrader, op.cit. 93-95 No. 44 pls. 62-67.

131. Cf. JHS 49 1929, 67 fig. 18, 69 fig. 21.

132. Cf. SCE IV 2, 119-120, 122, 124.

133. Cf. CVAOxford 1, 10-11, III 1 pl. 4.7-8, CVABritishMuseum, 4, 8 III I c pl. 37.5 a-b, JHS 49 1929, 74-75.

134. Cp. C. Blinkenberg, Knidia, Berlin 1933, 75-76 figs. 17-22, 95 fig. 39.

135. P.J. Riis, Griechen in Phönizien, Madrider Beiträge 8, Mainz 1982, 237-260.

136. M.-L. Buhl, L'origine des sarcophages anthropoïdes phéniciens en pierre, Atti del I Congresso Internazionale di Studi Fenici e Punici I, Rome 1983, 199-202.

137. ActaArch 48 1977, 139-154, ActaArch 49 1978, 239-240.

138. Det Kgl. Danske Videnskabernes Selskabs Skrifter 6th ser. IV 2, Copenhagen 1895, 59-91.

CONCORDANCE OF NUMBERS

Inventory	Catalogue
ABb 139	12, 13
ABb 241	80
ABb 242	72, 78, 79, 82, 83, 84
ABb 320	14
697	74
699	77
1511	57
1624	9
2125	71
2126	60, 75, 76
2127	81
2298	4
2299	3
3000	1
3001	2
3729	73
4695	8
4696	11
4697	10
4698	6
4699	5
5037	70
7061	7
7673	52
7674	20
7675	55
7676	29
10423	49
10424	50
10425	42
10426	51
10427	54
10428	19
10429	58
10430	45
10431	53
10432	18
10433	59
10434	16
10435	56

Inventory	Catalogue
10436	43
10437	44
10438	48
10439	46
10440	47
10441	31
10442	66
10443	21
10444	63
10445	62
10446	61
10447	64
10448	65
10449	68
10450	32
10451	33
10452	67
10453	23
10454	28
10455	24
10456	27
10457	25
10458	26
10459	30
10460	35
10461	36
10462	39
10463	40
10464	41
10465	37
10466	69
10467	22
11326	17
11327	15
11328	34
11329	38
13431	85
14384	86

LIST OF PROVENIENCES

(Figures refer to the catalogue)